AN AERIAL ARCHAEOLOGIST'S LOGBOOK, 1970-1995

sidestonepress

AN AERIAL ARCHAEOLOGIST'S LOGBOOK, 1970-1995

100 Air Photographs from Northern Britain

D.W. HARDING

Published by Sidestone Press, Leiden
www.sidestone.com
E-mail: info@sidestone.nl
Phone: (+31)(0)71-7370131

Lay-out & cover design: Sidestone Press
Photograph cover: Gurness (Plate 48), photo by Dennis Harding
Frontispiece: The Standing Stones at Calanais, Lewis, focus of a late Neolithic ceremonial landscape.

ISBN 978-94-6426-398-5 (softcover)
ISBN 978-94-6426-399-2 (hardcover)
ISBN 978-94-6426-400-5 (PDF e-book)

DOI: 10.59641/i9l5f6g7h8

Contents

List of Figures

List of Colour Plates

33. Broomside, Co. Durham, ditched enclosure.
34. Brandon, Co. Durham, ditched enclosure.
35a. Whitecraig, East Lothian, pit-alignment and ditched enclosures.
35b. Whitecraig, East Lothian, double pit-alignment and palisaded enclosure.
35c. Whitecraig, East Lothian, pit-alignment and linear ditches.
36. Whitelaw Hill, East Lothian, pit-alignment and ditched enclosure.
37. Eilean Breaban, Loch Tay.
38. Mary's Distaff, Loch Tay.
39. Craggan, Loch Tay.
40. Dall Bay, Loch Tay.
41. Bandry, Loch Lomond.
42. Cameron Bay, Loch Lomond.
43. Milton Morenish, Loch Tay.
44. Fearnan Hotel, Loch Tay.
45. Mill Cairn, Loch Lomond.
46. Strathcashel Point, Loch Lomond.
47a. Loch an Duin, Shader, Lewis.
47b. Loch an Duin, Shader, Lewis.
48. Gurness, Mainland, Orkney, broch village.
49. Midhowe, Rousay, Orkney, broch village.
50. Loch an Duna, Bragar, Lewis, island broch.
51a. Borve, Lewis, broch.
51b. Borve, Lewis, broch, from *c.* 300 feet.
52. Iona abbey, Inner Hebrides.
53. Whitby, North Yorkshire.

Preface

This collection of air photographs, taken over a period of twenty-five years from 1970, when I learned to fly at Sunderland Flying Club, represents a personal selection out of many thousands taken of those photographs that I believe are archaeologically meaningful and which reflect something of the standard of air photography to which we aspired. Before the advent of digital photography there was no way of knowing whether an image was good or bad until it had been developed and printed, often days later, so that results could be a lottery. Weather conditions could change between take-off and arrival at the target, wind could cause the aircraft to drift off the intended orbit, engine vibration in steep turns could result in blurred images and simple errors on the part of the photographer could further contribute to poor results. In Britain a fundamental problem is moisture in the atmosphere in suspension, resulting in a haze from reflected light. On many sunny days, when one can look up from ground level to an apparently cloudless sky, looking down from a thousand feet that ground is barely visible through the haze. Telephoto lenses plainly make no difference in terms of clarity: the only solution was to fly low, with all the attendant risks (and regulations) of doing so.

In concentrating principally upon Iron Age or Roman period sites I am only too aware that I might be accused of narrow-minded period specialism, in contrast to the late Professor Norman McCord's approach, in which the Tyne docks were accorded as high a priority as Hadrian's Wall. Norman was an historian and industrial archaeologist, and his recording of industrial monuments was timely. Had I been an independent researcher of private means in the tradition of Alexander Keiller I might well have adopted a more catholic and certainly more self-indulgent philosophy, but I was employed to research the Iron Age of Northern Britain, so that was my primary concern. This is not to say that I was insensitive to sites of other periods that represented important landmarks in our island's history. I therefore have included just three sites out of many possibilities that fall into that category on opposite sides of my flying circuit, Iona (Pl. 52) in the west and Whitby (Pl. 53) in the east. And, of course, Calanais, where the University of Edinburgh had its 200-acre archaeological field centre, adjacent to the Standing Stones (frontispiece), was focal to my research for many years.

Having become interested in air photography when, as temporary Assistant Keeper in the Ashmolean Museum in 1965-6, I was in charge of Major Allen's Collection of air photographs, I very soon determined that the best way to achieve desired results was to learn to fly myself, since it was quite difficult to persuade a commercial pilot to position the aircraft to best advantage photographically, even if he (and I never had a lady instructor or commercial pilot) understood what it was that he was supposed to be looking at. Since it was impractical to fly the plane and take the photographs at the same time, it was necessary, once in the correct orbit, to have a co-pilot to operate the controls while I took the pictures. I was fortunate in having several co-pilots who fulfilled that role in exemplary fashion, but Denis Ord from Sunderland was quite exceptional in sensing the very moment that I was about to take the photograph, applying a fraction of rudder to lift the wing of the Cessna that otherwise at steep angles threatened to dip into the picture. The result was that our circuits around a target tended to be a series of skids rather than balanced orbit, which meant with a gravity-feed fuel system that by the end of the sortie the starboard fuel tank was rather more depleted than the port, potentially presenting problems in a left-hand circuit, turning on to base leg and on to finals.

In these days of digital photography it is perhaps appropriate to say something about the equipment that we used. All our cameras would now be classified as 'retro-models'. In my Durham days I used a Mamiya that took 120 or 220 size film for black and white, and a Pentax single lens reflex camera for colour. I used zoom lenses where appropriate, and very occasionally a huge 300mm telephoto lens mounted on a cut-down rifle-stock and fired by cable release from the trigger. It was not very practical, since it was very difficult from a moving platform to train it accurately on the target, and its best service proved to be when my flying and digging colleague Peter Scott took it on a safari holiday in Africa to photograph wild life from a safe distance. In Edinburgh I used a motor driven Hasselblad, allegedly the same model as was used in the American lunar landings. It had the advantage of magazines that would take up to seventy shots of 70mm film, so that, with extra magazines already loaded before the flight, minimal time was wasted changing film in the air. The disadvantage was that the camera was extremely heavy, and in a four-hour sortie took its toll on the arms. Its batteries, which were very expensive to replace, were also prone to going flat in flight, with no provision for a manual over-ride. On one occasion when they failed right at the outset of the photographic session I made an unannounced landing at Brunton in Northumberland, where the farmer was a club member who used the former RAF runway on his land, in order to recharge the batteries in his kitchen. For colour by this time I was using a Nikon SLR as well as a Pentax, both of which gave years of trouble-free service.

In my experience there were two major problems in archaeological air photography. The first was positioning the aircraft in the right place, that is low enough and steep enough over the target to show the important detail. Recording that detail was obviously improved by using large-format cameras. The second was getting enough contrast into the picture to show what the archaeologist was interested in. The first was achieved by flying the plane oneself, since no-one else would willingly be so foolhardy. The second was fundamentally dependent upon the weather. Far too many poor air photographs have been taken by archaeologists who did not have the patience to wait for conditions to be right, and by all of us who found that conditions had deteriorated en route to the target. One tip that certainly helped for black and white photography was to use a X2 yellow filter, but not to double the exposure in compensation, instead doubling the development time. This certainly had the effect of heightening contrast, but there was always the risk that, if one changed to colour film in flight, forgetting to remove the filter resulted in an expensively lurid waste of film and flying opportunity. Now of course errors of commission can in some measure be compensated for by computer enhancement, and a very few of the photographs here reproduced have been treated this way. I should nevertheless record my gratitude for their efforts over the years in redeeming my photographs to the photographic technicians at Durham and Edinburgh, Tom Middlemass and Joe Rock respectively.

For the record, my flying training was undertaken at my own expense, as was the great bulk of my air-photographic flying. I nevertheless acknowledge with gratitude small research grants from the Durham University Excavation Committee, and from the former Department of the Environment Air- Photographic Committee's annual funds for air photography. I received support also from the erstwhile Fieldwork Fund of the Department of Archaeology of the University of Edinburgh, and from the erstwhile Royal Commission on the Ancient and Historical Monuments of Scotland.

Finally, as to choice of aircraft, in common with most of the archaeological community, I used a Cessna 172 for the most part. In Durham days I did have a share in a small, high-winged plane called a Brochet, designed after the War by a Frenchman, Marcel Brochet, for the Paris air show, of which only about half a dozen were ever built. After it had been rebuilt by Denis Ord I accompanied him on its test flight. My recollection was that it stalled at just thirty miles an hour, which left us idly speculating whether, in a strong wind directly down the runway, we might not have landed it backwards, in a fashion emulating the late comedian Tony Hancock's efforts in the film *Those Magnificent Men in their Flying Machines.* We never did. Ours was then the last of the marque still flying; eventually it joined the others as a crash statistic.

Dennis Harding,
Gullane,
Christmas, 2014

* * * * *

Ten years have elapsed since I prepared this volume for publication. In that time the use of drones for aerial survey and photography has rendered conventional air photography obsolescent, having the advantage for photographing specific sites of allowing the archaeologist to position his equipment at the optimum location and to wait for optimum conditions, without the uncertainty and expense of flying an aircraft to a location remote from base, only to find that the weather has deteriorated and frustrated the exercise. For survey of more remote landscapes, as in the Western Isles of Scotland, an aircraft still doubtless has its value, but drones unquestionably have made local aerial photography infinitely more practical. Whilst the archaeological topics and issues discussed here remain fundamental, therefore, in other respects the present volume now assumes the status of a historical document, and accordingly the text of 2014 has not been revised. It simply records principles and practices that were once basic to archaeological fieldwork, but are now largely part of archaeological history, as shortly will be its author.

Dennis Harding,
East Linton,
February, 2025

1

Principles and Practice of Aerial Archaeology

Archaeological air photography is not an end in itself: it is simply a tool, and a highly effective one, in the larger study of landscape archaeology. It has the important advantage of providing a detached perspective on the often complex and superimposed patterns created by generations of human settlement, which at ground level may be too complex to be readily understood. O. G. S. Crawford's analogy of the cat's eye view of a patterned carpet by comparison with the human's view graphically illustrated this simple fact. There is no mystique about air photography; nothing appears when viewed from above which is not there when viewed from the ground. The object of the exercise is simply to use that detached perspective, combined with the variable factors of lighting, seasonal change in vegetational growth, soil moisture variability and a range of related considerations, to produce a record of sub-surface or low relief features in the landscape that accentuates those features to maximum advantage.

The second mistaken belief, of which students of archaeology have frequently to be disabused, is that air photography is something that the field archaeologist invariably does prior to excavation, in order to discover a site worthy of his attentions. This, one is told, is an expensive business, which limits its applicability. Excavators may occasionally commission air surveys, but this is very much an optional extra. The first step is to consult the *existing* record of air photographs, since, cost aside, there is no guarantee that the conditions at the time of excavation would be conducive to good air-photographic results. Searching existing air-photographic records therefore would be a standard part of pre-excavation planning, together with other relevant archive searches.

It is often supposed that a helicopter would be an ideal platform for archaeological air photography, given its capacity to hover around the optimal viewpoint over the target. In fact most helicopter pilots would prefer to fly forward into wind than to hover, when the machine is at its most vulnerable, and in any event the level of vibration in hovering is counter-productive to the best photographic results, even using a fast shutter speed. On one occasion I used a Westland Wessex, sitting strapped to the floor with my feet over the ledge of the open door, which gave an excellent view of the ground beneath; but the vibration, and more especially the shimmering exhaust from the aircraft's engines, produced an unfortunate blur across most of the resultant pictures. Perhaps a smaller helicopter of the bubble-on-stick variety would be more suitable, but the cost still tends to be prohibitive for most private or academic users. At various times friends suggested to me the use of microlight aircraft or kites (drones would now be a much better option), but I preferred the conventional single-engined high-wing monoplane of the Cessna 172 variety. It may not have been the most exhilarating flying experience, but it afforded good visibility of the ground, had just sufficient room if required for three persons with equipment, and in certain models had a sufficient range to reach remoter survey areas without too great a risk of running out of fuel. The latter consideration was a very real one when survey in the Northern or Western Isles was being planned, and where significant stretches of

Figure 1: 'Big Geordie' operating at an opencast mining site at Widdrington, Northumberland.

open water had to be crossed. Its handling, especially when landing in a strong cross-wind or with full-flap, may have been like flying a council contractor's wheelbarrow, but it was reasonably tolerant of the sort of abuses to which the average flying club membership subjected it.

Taking the photograph may not be an end in itself, but to publish a volume of air photographs might appear to endorse that impression. Of course a good air photograph is a source of satisfaction, and one perhaps too seldom achieved in proportion to the effort expended. Nothing was more depressing than the annual conferences of archaeological air photographers parading their mediocre images like postage-stamps ('and here's another, and another..' as one respected practitioner used to intone), without any apparent appreciation of the need to understand and interpret the evidence depicted in terms of past human settlement patterns and their significance. Once the photograph has been taken, the next stage in the exercise is the transcription and rectification of the data visible on it into mapped form, to be added to the accumulating evidence of previous sorties in which different archaeological features may have been revealed under different conditions. The product should then be a composite plan which can be integrated with information derived from other forms of remote-sensing or ground-based survey.

Air survey plainly has an invaluable role to play in locating sites, or in monitoring the condition of known sites, in landscapes like upland Britain or in the remoter Northern and Western Isles, where access over land and water would be laborious and time-consuming. But it can also be an invaluable aid in monitoring development and in providing an archaeological input into the planning process. In the 1970s, when 'rescue archaeology' was in its infancy, air photography had an important role to play in identifying sites that might be threatened by new activities like opencast mining, the capacity for destruction of which may be judged by the scale of machinery employed, like the then National Coal Board's 'Big Geordie' (Fig. 1), a 3000-tonne walking dragline that could shift well over 100,000 tonnes of overburden a day. Development was not just a threat to hitherto unknown sites detected by air photography. Major upstanding monuments, including hillforts like the Dunion in Roxburghshire (Fig. 2), Kaimes, Midlothian and Clatchard Craig in Fife were completely obliterated by quarrying, while even Traprain Law in East Lothian has been partly quarried away over the years.

Whilst aerial archaeology unquestionably involves certain specialist skills which make it in practice a distinct sub-section of the discipline, in principle we are all archaeologists, whether our particular proclivity is to

Figure 2: the Dunion, Roxburghshire, in course of obliteration by quarrying.

take to the air or to don a dry-suit and plunge the depths. The segregation of aerial archaeology, like underwater archaeology, from the mainstream of field archaeology has sometimes in the past been a limiting factor in the maximization of resources and effort. It is especially surprising that geophysical survey until recently was not deployed more regularly as an obvious follow-up to air-survey, since it affords a cost-effective and non-destructive means of amplifying the information obtained from the air, and securing its location spatially on the ground.

Air photography of course is not the exclusive preserve of archaeologists. Aerial reconnaissance was initially pioneered during the First World War for military purposes, since when it has been exploited for a great variety of military, commercial, research and governmental purposes, with satellite surveillance as just the latest and highest-tec application. Professional air survey generally entails taking an overlapping sequence of *vertical* air photographs, requiring an aircraft suitably adapted, for the purpose of creating overlapping stereo sequences. The advantage of oblique photography is that it can highlight under optimum conditions significant features that are flattened in many vertical photographs. Commercial or military verticals are in any event frequently taken from too great a height and under less than optimal conditions for archaeological purposes. The advantage of vertical cover is that it is more readily transcribed into mapped form, though irregularities in terrain can still result in significant distortion. Obliques by definition require rectification if the information is to be transcribed on to maps or larger-scale plans. The photographs in this collection are therefore necessarily all technically obliques, even though on occasion the angle of obliquity, through accident or design, may have approximated to the vertical.

Crop-marks

Archaeological air photography in lowland Britain is not invariably but predominantly photography of crop-marks. In upland Britain this is not the case, reflecting the nature of the landscape and the prevailing agricultural priorities. In those regions, like the Lothian and Berwickshire plain, where arable agriculture remains predominant, the factors determining the recognition of crop-marks are comparable to those of Southern Britain. Ancient settlement almost invariably has involved some kind of intrusion into the subsoil or into bedrock in the form of pits or ditches or even large post-holes, all of which may show up because, once the ground is disturbed, the overlying crop will reflect that sub-surface disturbance. Even though the ground has been leveled by generations of later agriculture, the infilling of

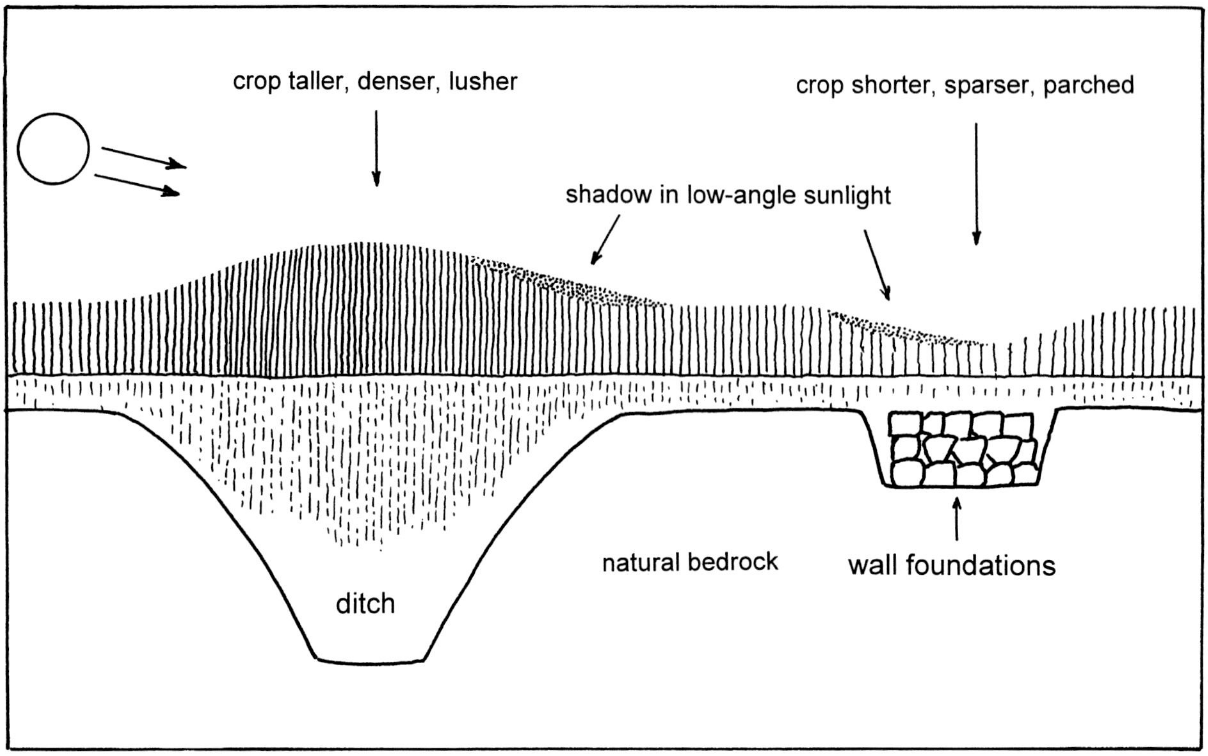

Figure 3: principles of crop-mark archaeology.

former pits or ditches will be of different consistency from the undisturbed sub-soil or underlying geology, and this will be reflected in the surface vegetation. As a rule of thumb, over ditches we may expect a taller, lusher crop and over stony structures such as buildings or roads a sparser, thinner, more thread-bare crop (Fig. 3).

Particularly in dry summers, when there is a significant *soil moisture deficit,* crops growing over the deeper humic soil of a pit or ditch will draw moisture from a greater depth, while crops growing on building foundations, like their Biblical counterparts on stony ground, will be more stunted and parch out sooner. Crops growing in such contrasting situations will show a differential colour and growth rate from those growing over the surrounding areas, particularly in the ripening stages before harvest. In practice crops growing over sub-surface ditches or pits may appear as a darker green against a neutral green background in the green stage, or later as a dark golden brown against a more neutral, yellow golden colour when ripened, both being rendered on a black-and-white image as a comparatively darker line. This principle is here illustrated by the Neolithic *cursus*, possible causewayed enclosure and associated features at Hasting Hill, Sunderland (Fig. 4), photographed in the early 1970s before major development of the area, the date of which was subsequently confirmed by trial excavations by Durham University. Conversely, crops over stony features will bleach out much more quickly, generally observable as a lighter mark within the neutral background, as illustrated particularly well in the photograph of the *vicus* settlement at Piercebridge (Pl. 1). Whilst the roads and building foundations show as lighter marks, however, we may note that, where sections were excavated by Peter Scott in the early 1970s across the main line of Dere Street, the infilled trenches nevertheless show as darker lines across the road.

These, however, are only generalizations, and a variety of circumstances can create deviant patterns. In conditions of extreme drought, for example, even cereal crops over ditched features can bleach out in a reversal of the standard effect. An example was the native settlement at Larberry Pastures, Stockton-on-Tees (Pl. 2), where a roundhouse can be seen inside an irregular enclosure, and where all the ditched features are showing as lighter reversal marks, the taller crop having been beaten down by storm and wind to produce an effect not unlike the sparse growth over sub-surface walls or roads.

In the past twenty years or so there has been a significant decline in the effectiveness of crop-mark photography for archaeological purposes, principally as a result of improved agricultural technology. In essence, the archaeologist benefited from the enhanced growth differential induced by drought conditions, whereas the farmer, by application of appropriate crop treatments, is keen to reduce the differential to improve yields. In

Figure 4: Neolithic *cursus*, enclosure and ring-ditches at Hasting Hill, Sunderland.

consequence, more sophisticated methods of monitoring crop conditions and of countering effects that might adversely affect yields have progressively eliminated the prospects that air photography will ever again capture some of the more dramatic effects of seasons like 1976.

The principles and causes of crop-marks are not restricted to features of archaeological significance, but can apply equally to sub-surface features induced by geological processes or by agricultural practices. Most commonly, the differential moisture levels induced by field drains will create a distinctive pattern in the crop which is readily distinguishable from patterns of archaeological significance, as exemplified at Easter Muirdean in Roxburghshire (Pl. 3) (though the archaeologist hardly expects the intervention of forestry to point out the presence of the ditched enclosure!). More problematical are the reflected patterns of geological effects, such as periglacial frost-cracking, which may easily be confused with early agricultural field-systems or enclosures. In the latter case the 'crazy-paving' effect is indicative of a natural origin, but in some cases where natural features are interspersed with genuine archaeological traces, distinguishing the two may be more contentious. A possible example is the site at Thornybank, Dalkeith (Pl. 4), where some of the spidery curves look suspiciously natural, while other linear features could be trackways. The fact that the field was adjacent to a later Iron Age cemetery site excavated in advance of construction of the Dalkeith by-pass link to the Edinburgh southern ring-road could explain some of the smaller patches on the photograph, so that a combination of archaeological and natural features is not improbable.

Soil-marks

A second category of air-photographic images is soil-marks, which will show to best effect in autumn when the land is ploughed or again in spring when fresh ploughing takes place. These marks tend to be more difficult to spot, not only because the weather conditions for flying and photography can be adverse when ploughing takes place, but because it only takes a day or two of rain for clear distinctions in the soil to be smudged and obscured. Among the clearest examples of soil-mark settlements in our area are ditched enclosures, like that at Ovingham, within the Newcastle airport approach zone, an enclosure of Iron Age or Romano-British date, revealed by the darker tones of their ditch filling, and contiguous lighter colour of the soil where the bank formerly stood (Pl. 5). The bank has evidently been constructed using material quarried from the ditch, including sterile, natural subsoil or bedrock from the ditch bottom which formed the core of the bank. Despite leveling through agricultural activity over the centuries, the residual difference between the bank core and the ditch silts still survives sufficiently to show the outline of the enclosure earthworks. The effects of ploughing may displace or distort the original outline, but hardly sufficiently to conceal its location and identification.

Extant earthworks

In contrast to crop-mark or soil-mark photography, which may result in the discovery of hitherto unknown sites, the point of photographing sites that survive as extant earthworks, amenable to examination and survey on the ground, may be less obvious. As a matter of practicality, that same remoteness which has resulted in the survival of archaeological remains may inhibit access for survey and research, especially in the remoter Highlands and Islands, for example (Pl. 6), where air survey, notwithstanding its expense, can be a cost-effective and time-saving alternative to weeks of ground survey with the aid of argocats and boats. In fact, in many upland regions the survival of relatively slight settlement traces, like the palisade trenches of later prehistoric homesteads, is extremely marginal after two and a half thousand years, and may seem no more substantial than sheep-tracks through the grass or heather. These fugitive patterns are much clearer when viewed from the detached perspective of the aerial archaeologist, and in consequence air photographs can be an invaluable adjunct to ground survey. This was particularly well illustrated in the survey of the patterns of 'cord-rig' agriculture in the Borders.

The traces of this form of agricultural system, first recognized in the early 1980s and dating from the mid-first millennium BC, comprise rigs no more than a metre apart, with furrows which on excavation have proved barely a foot or eighteen inches in depth and no more across, the product of spade cultivation rather than ploughing. On the surface the traces are so faint as only to be visible when vegetation is at its barest, and even then trying to plot the patterns in plan is a recipe for insanity, and will test the patience and credulity of the most tolerant team of surveyors (Fig. 5a). Again, air photographs provide the vital element of a detached perspective, and have generally been used in close conjunction with ground survey to produce the best approximation to an accurate, planned rendering of this highly elusive archaeological phenomenon. Dating remains problematical, but cord-rig regularly occurs in association with palisaded settlements and roundhouses of ring-ditch type, both of which appear to be current from the earlier Iron Age. Cord-rig from Woden Law is here illustrated from among the outworks, where it appears to be secondary to the linear earthworks, though still probably the product of Iron Age occupation, and between the banks outwith the hillfort's north-eastern sector, where the rigs are accentuated by a light fall of snow (Fig. 5c). The angle of sunlight is the key factor in photographing extant earthworks from the air. A mid-day sun will flatten most features into oblivion, whereas an early morning or late evening oblique light can throw even minimal features into sharp relief. Whilst this sounds like a simple enough formula, in practice it may be harder to achieve. In parts of the Border hills, by the time the sun is low enough to register the minimal traces we are concerned with, shadows from higher adjacent hills may have blotted out the site altogether.

Assuming that the angle of sunlight is at its optimum, it is still necessary for the photographer to position himself or herself at the best angle relative to the incident light. Following the novice's advice that the sun should be over your shoulder will hardly here produce the desired effect, since that angle will not include the cast shadows which are vital to throwing the slight earthworks into relief. Turn through 180 degrees to maximize the shadows, and the camera will be facing directly into low sunlight, with all the risks that entails. An angle to either side of the axis of sunlight produces the optimum effect, towards the sun, but not directly at it. In consequence many photographic sorties had to be conducted in late afternoon or early evening, returning to base just before sunset. Because the prevailing wind is south-westerly, the majority of airfields in Britain have their principal runways oriented from north-east to south-west. So when the pilot turns from base leg on to final approach at around five hundred feet he finds himself staring directly into the setting sun on the end of the runway. Judging the round-out in such circumstances was more than usually hazardous, a triumph of good fortune over airmanship.

Extant earthworks are best photographed when the surface vegetation is minimal, between late autumn and early spring. They may however be greatly enhanced, as at Woden Law (Pl. 7), by a light dusting of snow or heavy frost, in much the same way that fingerprints are accentuated by a light dusting of powder. In the Cheviots a light fall of snow is generally a contradiction in terms, a heavier fall simply obscuring the subject altogether. The effect can sometimes be a dazzling palimpsest of features, as at Blakehope in Northumberland (Fig. 6), where the auxiliary fort and larger, earlier temporary camp are overlain by medieval and later agriculture. For that reason, though some photographs have benefited from snow-enhancement,

Figure 5a: Woden Law, Hownam, Roxburghshire, cord-rig agriculture at ground level

Figure 5b: Woden Law, Hownam, Roxburghshire, cord-rig among outer banks.

Figure 5c: Woden Law, Hownam, Roxburghshire, cord-rig between 'siege-works' Z and outer linear bank W outside hillfort to the north-east. The photograph in this instance was taken from around 300 feet on 70mm film.

Figure 6: Blakehope, Northumberland, Roman auxiliary fort and temporary camp with overlying medieval rig-and-furrow under snow.

some of the best are those taken in early morning after a heavy frost. The two conditions may be compared at Hut Knowe, Hownam, Roxburghshire (Pl. 8a,b).

Some very fugitive archaeological features like cord-rig required photography from close range to reveal them to best effect. In fact, my personal experience was that in some cases 35mm film gave insufficient resolution to show the required detail, and 70mm was to be preferred. The optimum height for photographing some of the smaller enclosures or fainter agricultural traces could be as low as three hundred feet, which in the Cheviots could be unpredictably turbulent. Simply using telephoto lenses from a greater height was no solution, since the haze which is endemic in the British climate, caused by moisture or particles in suspension that reflect low-angle sunlight, invariably cast a veil over the target that telephoto lenses cannot penetrate. The only assured way of obtaining optimum results is to photograph at low level. In the case of the Cheviots survey, an added hazard was conflicting traffic on military exercises, contour flying the narrow valleys and heading for the Otterburn range.

Underwater sites

Air photography of underwater or wetland archaeological sites is once again not a major concern of field archaeologists in lowland Britain, but in a country with several thousand inland lochs as an integral part of the landscape available for settlement, notably of crannogs or lakeside dwellings, and as principal arteries of communication in early times, it clearly has considerable potential. Given that the considerable extent of Scotland's coastline is also subject to marine erosion, the capacity of air survey to monitor and record coastal settlement is equally important.

Photographing crannogs is not, of course, simply a matter of turning up with a plane and a camera, any more than it is in any other branch of archaeological air photography. Ideally the water needs to be not just calm but still, since the slightest ripple on the surface reflects light and conceals the sub-surface features. Equally the water needs to be clear enough to see structures two or three metres below the surface, which is unlikely to be the case if recent rain storms have resulted in heavy run-off from the catchment system. In short, the archaeologist is demanding conditions which are hardly typical of the central Highlands. Even in the Outer Hebrides, where the surrounding terrain is in general much less hilly, wind and rain will have the effect of disturbing the silts on the loch bed, which are frequently disproportionately deep compared to the shallow depth of surface water. A major factor in inland lochs like Loch Tay is the seasonal rise and fall of the water level, which can be several metres, so that in general summer photography is more likely to catch the tip of crannogs breaking the surface or to record the maximum extent of their underwater plan, even allowing for the fact that water-levels today are controlled.

As with land survey, understanding the topography of settlement is important in locating crannogs. Within major mainland lochs like Loch Tay and Loch Awe, the wave fetch over ten miles and more of open water can be considerable, so that crannogs were frequently sited where small inlets or bays afforded a measure of shelter from the prevailing weather. Equally the topography itself determines the potential for crannog settlement. A steep incline from hillside to loch without break of slope leaves no possibility of crannog construction. The most likely location is therefore where there is a shelf below a few metres of water before the contours drop steeply away, so that the crannog can be sited sufficiently far from the shore to afford a measure of protection, but close enough for convenient access by causeway. Air survey therefore means cruising along the shoreline at the legal minimum distance of 500 feet on the look-out for likely locations. The target is smaller than many archaeological sites, but they are also known to occur in pairs or small groups, not necessarily of sites in contemporary use, but sometimes seemingly successive, as in the case of the Dall Island sites in Loch Tay or the island duns at Shader in Lewis.

Transcription and plotting

We have stressed that air photography of archaeological sites is not an end in itself, but just one (very effective) technique for enhancing the known data-base of sites and monuments, to which field survey or ground walking by amateur or professional teams alike is an equally important contributor. Transcription of the information contained on air photographs and rectification from oblique image to a scaled plan are plainly essential if ground survey is accurately to locate a site. Rectification of data from oblique air photographs was formerly done by mechanical methods, the so-called paper-strip method or Mobius network method that have been described in detail by Wilson (1982; 2000) and Riley (1987). Laborious as it was, and not nearly as accurate as computer rectification, it nevertheless served adequately for the purposes of academic synthesis, even if less reliably for the purposes of field investigation. Even with the benefits of computer transcription, it must be remembered that the results are only as good as the quality of interpretation, which even undertaken by experienced archaeologists remains a subjective exercise. Particularly where genuine archaeological features are obscured by or merged with geological patterns or more recent agricultural marks there is often no certainly correct interpretation, and it is probable that no two archaeologists would independently produce the same transcription. Add to this the fact that multiple photographs of the same site may have been taken on different occasions and under different conditions, and it becomes clear that the end product can only be the best composite evaluation of the available data, subject always to revision in the light of subsequent sorties.

Transcribing and plotting the results of upland photography of extant earthworks is not nearly as straightforward as it might be for crop-mark archaeology. Whereas crop-marks are usually found where the landscape canvas is a plane, if not level surface, upland sites can straddle a much more irregular topography, resulting in foreshortening and distortion of the image. Furthermore, the basic requirement of several fixed points on the ground, corresponding to fixed points on the base map on to which the archaeological features are to be transcribed, is seldom met in high-contour terrain, where any form of fencing or landmark other than intermittent plantations is a rarity. On the other hand, where the features being photographed are part of, or adjacent to an upstanding earthwork which itself has been subject to accurate ground survey, then of course it is relatively easy to match the additional data from air photographs to that basic survey. Indeed, the fundamental purpose of our intensive survey of the Roxburghshire Cheviots was to enhance the known data-base, derived essentially from the published *Inventory* (1956) of the Royal Commission on the Ancient and Historical Monuments of Scotland and greatly supplemented by additional data in the National Monuments Record of Scotland, to a level which is seldom attainable in regions where modern development has been more intrusive. In broad perspective, this might be compared to the use of air-photographic data in the study of the Danebury landscape in a lowland context in Southern Britain.

The objectives of archaeological air photography therefore can be several. At the most basic level it can be deployed as an instrument in site discovery, simply adding to the documented record of known sites, whether for research purposes or for the purposes of monitoring the possible implications of development. At another level it can be used for intensive survey of a specific area in the hope of increasing *qualitatively* our understanding of the settlement patterns of the past through the maximization of all traces of activity in the landscape. Third, it may have a role in tackling specific problems in relation to individual sites or classes of monuments. Publicly-funded agencies are likely to be most concerned with the first of these objectives, which is not to say that they are not concerned with the academic evaluation of the data recovered and recorded. Academic archaeologists are more likely to be concerned with the second or third objectives, with research projects targeted at specific academic issues.

Finally, having stressed the advantages and benefits of air photography as a means of archaeological survey, it is only fair to point out its limitations. At the most basic level the limitations of access, over zones of restricted airspace, are self-evident. Constraints imposed by land-use, such as afforestation or forms of agriculture which are not amenable to revealing sub-surface traces of archaeological sites (though infra-red and related techniques may be deployed to advantage), may also throw archaeological distributions into imbalance. But even where such constraints do not intervene, it does not follow that archaeological sites will always appear more meaningfully from the air than on the ground. The potential of air photography has its inherent limitations. If the pre-eminent advantage lies in its detached perspective, enabling a site to be observed and studied in its spatial landscape context, its limitation is that the prominence of site location or the monumentality of the structure itself is often diminished from the air. Nowhere is the environmental context of a site more graphically demonstrated than in the photographs of promontory or cliff-edge sites in Shetland, for example, but equally the monumentality of major surviving brochs, like Mousa in Shetland or Carloway in Lewis is much more emphatically displayed on the ground, as of course it was originally intended to be. This basic truth is one reason why air survey should not be conducted in isolation from ground survey or other forms of site detection and investigation. All have their roles in contemporary field archaeology, and can be most profitably conducted in association.

2

Native and Roman in Northern Britain

The northern frontier of Roman Britain

It might seem improbable that air photography could cast much new light on a field of study like the Roman northern frontier, so well researched over the past hundred years and more, and represented on the ground by upstanding monuments as impressive as Hadrian's Wall and its associated forts. In large measure this is true; some of the photographs presented here simply display in striking visual form what is clear enough on the ground, like the well-known site of Housesteads on Hadrian's Wall (Fig. 7).

Figure 7: Housesteads, Northumberland.

Figure 8: Washing Well, Whickham, Co. Durham.

Particularly clear here is the Military Way emerging from the west gate of the fort, and flanked by small rectangular paddocks or enclosures on either side. During my years in Durham I photographed many of the sites on and in the hinterland of the Wall, and these are archived in the Department of Archaeology at the University of Durham.

Spectacular as it is, Hadrian's Wall and its major hinterland forts nevertheless represent only part of the story of the Roman northern frontier, and in particular evidence for the pre-Hadrianic frontier in northern England and Scotland leaves many questions unanswered. The discovery in 1970 by Professor Norman McCord (1971; 1972) of the substantial crop-mark fort at Washing Well, Whickham, Gateshead (Fig. 8), raised challenging questions regarding the eastern extension of the Stanegate frontier, and the possibility that it may have followed a course south of the river Tyne east of Corbridge. Clearly indicating a succession of timber structures, the details of the entrances indicated that these were permanent forts not temporary camps, though not yet built of stone, and therefore probably pre-Hadrianic. Likewise the realization as a result of quarrying at Piercebridge in the 1970s that the *vicus* so clearly visible in air photographs (Pl. 1) extended south of the Tees, together with more recent discoveries at Sedgefield, Co Durham, has raised the possibility that the civilian landscape in the frontier hinterland included settlements that approximated to small towns. Nevertheless, we often assume that more is known about the major frontier forts than is warranted by research. The fort and *vicus* at Old Carlisle have hardly been investigated in modern times (Fig. 9). The outline of the external settlement in particular is accentuated by the upcast from trenches dug in the course of stone robbing for later construction. Noticeably the line of the Roman road from Carlisle to the coast passes through the civilian settlement and is taken up by a later field boundary to the east and the modern A595 to the west (Fig. 9, a, b). A minor road leads from the *vicus* to the east gate of the fort. Other external buildings are visible north and east of the fort, but much of the south and west sides is overlain by later agriculture. A number of inscriptions from the site indicate occupation in the second and third centuries, but any evidence for the fort's earlier origins could only be recovered from

Figure 9a: Old Carlisle, Wigton, Cumbria, fort and *vicus*.

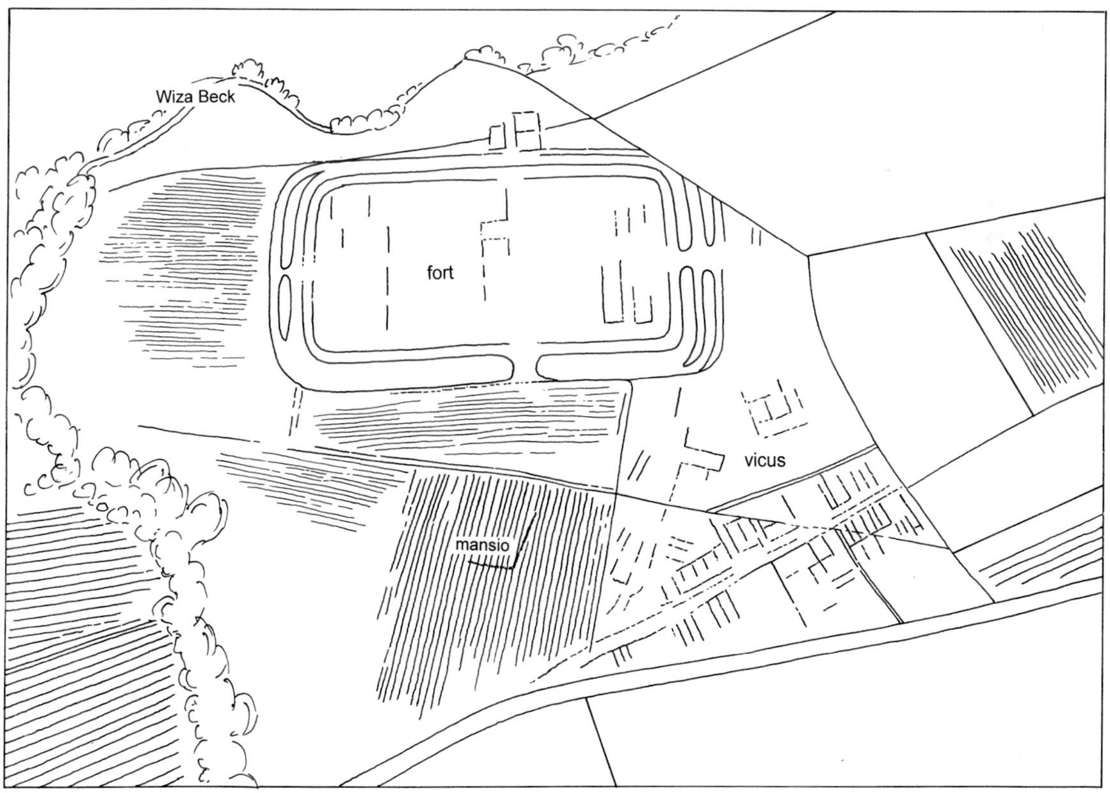

Figure 9b: Old Carlisle, Wigton, Cumbria, sketch plan of principal features.

Figure 10: Whitley Castle, near Alston, Cumbria, in oblique sunlight.

excavation. Systematic flying by Professor Barri Jones (Jones and Wooliscroft, 2001: Fig. 41) revealed a complex network of fields, trackways and farmsteads that made up the surrounding Romano-British landscape.

The site at Whitley Castle (Fig. 10) has been hailed as one of the best-preserved but least understood in Northern Britain. This is a striking example of a site that requires low-angle oblique sunlight to show its defences to best advantage. The fort, which stands alone on this isolated stretch of the South Tyne Valley, was occupied throughout the second and third centuries, and was probably located strategically to control the area's lead resources. Its siting, on a spur high on the west side of the valley, required modification of the normal rectangular outline into its distinctive rhomboidal form, while its multiple ramparts, especially strengthened on the uphill side to include no less than seven lines of defence, is unique among Roman forts. Internally, nevertheless, the arrangement of headquarters building, commandant's house, barracks and granaries apparently follows standard form. The minor Roman road known as the Maiden Way is visible east of the fort beneath later Medieval rig-and-furrow in the foreground of the photograph, with the road to it from the fort's east gate just detectable.

The major fort complex at Birrens is well-known (Fig. 11), comprising the low, extant walls of a fort that was occupied and successively re-modeled from Flavian through Hadrianic to the final Antonine occupation. More problematical are the adjacent crop-marks to the west, which include two separate triple-ditched enclosures as well as various internal features. The alignment of the main Roman road through Annandale on the larger of these enclosures suggests that they were not simply secondary additions, but somehow integral to the complex. Air photography comes into its own in the location of the more fugitive remains of Roman temporary camps, no lesser in area but with much less substantial defences than permanent forts. The pencil-thin outline of their ditches, and occasionally traces of their distinctive entrances with

Figure 11: Birrens, Dumfriesshire, fort with large annexe.

Figure 12: Birrens, Dumfriesshire, temporary camp.

protective curving *claviculae* or offset *tituli*, as at Birrens (Fig. 12), are tell-tale features.

In strict terms it is obviously not possible to read 'stratigraphy' from air photographs, but in some instances where crop-marks reveal a palimpsest of superimposed features it may be possible to infer a relative sequence. An example of this is the photograph of the civilian settlement outside the Roman fort at Piercebridge on the Tees (Fig. 13a,b; Pl. 1). The principal features in the Tofts Field are buildings aligned along roads, exemplifying the principle of crops

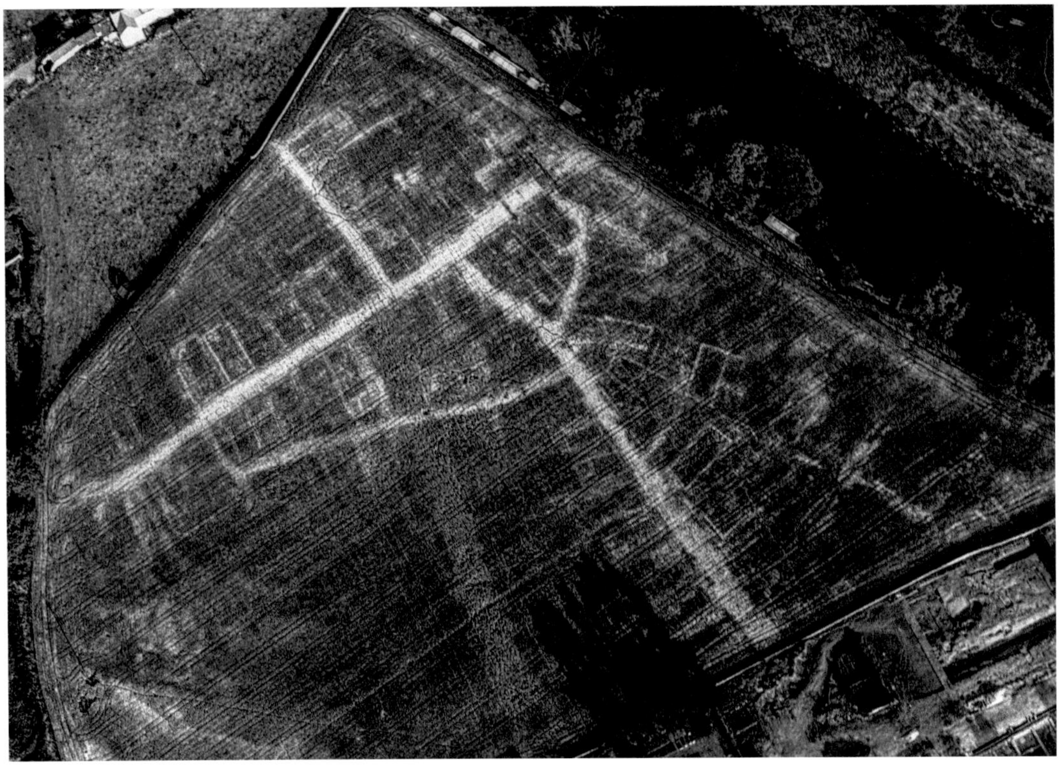

Figure 13a: the Tofts, Piercebridge, Dere street and *vicus* outside Roman fort.

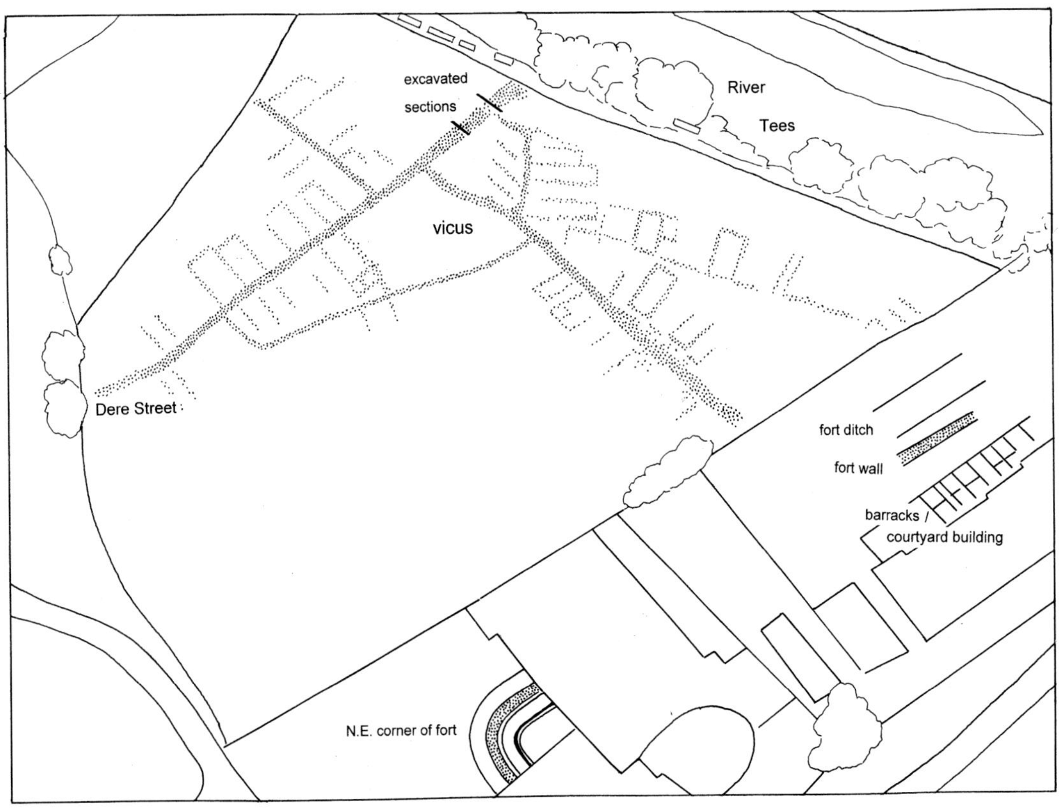

Figure 13b: the Tofts, Piercebridge, principal features from air photography and excavation.

bleaching out over stony foundations. The road leading from the east gate of the fort towards Dere Street is plain enough, but this road takes a curious turn just before it joins the major south-north road. This change of alignment was evidently a result of an earlier street, now only faintly visible with the buildings fronting on to it, following an alignment closer to the river, and possibly indicative of the location of the missing earlier fort. Excavations in the 1970s by Peter Scott (Cool and Mason, 2008) in various locations within the modern village, however, failed to detect any trace of an earlier fort, the existence of which therefore remains conjectural. At the same time he supervised excavations on the east side of the fort in advance of a housing development, which uncovered part of a courtyard building, previously interpreted as a barrack block, that is just visible within the eastern defences.

The existence of the villa enclosure at Holme House (Fig. 14), just above the flood-plain south of the Tees east of Piercebridge, had been known for some years from a series of air photographs taken by Professor J. K. St Joseph, which showed an approach road through an annexe on the east side of the enclosure that invited comparison with Major Allen's air photograph of the Ditchley, Oxfordshire, villa (Harding, 2020, Fig. 3.2A). But the early date of the settlement was not appreciated until excavation in advance of quarrying in 1969-70. The abandonment and dismantling of the villa by the end of the second century was more probably due to persistent flooding than to political disruptions over the frontier, and the discovery from the air of another enclosure, on the higher terrace overlooking the next bend of the Tees downstream (Pl. 9) suggests a possible location for the settlement's successor. Cool and Mason (2008: 297) alternatively suggested that the abandonment of the Holme House villa resulted from the expansion of Piercebridge as a garrison town at the end of the second century, an interpretation that is certainly more plausible than marauding Maeatae. For some years this was the best-documented northerly villa in the empire, until the site that had been identified from the air at Ingleby Barwick, Stockton-on-Tees (Fig. 15), likewise just south of the river and on the same latitude as Holme House, proved on excavation to be that of a winged corridor villa (Willis and Carne, 2013). Meantime, the quarrying of the adjacent fields south of the river at Piercebridge revealed the presence of a substantial Roman bridge (Fig. 16) and a substantial extension of the civilian settlement.

An interesting facet of Roman military practice in Northern Britain is the inferred re-use of Iron Age defensive camps as practice grounds for the use of artillery and assault techniques. At Woden Law (Pl. 7) the 'siege-works' comprise two separate elements, the double banks and triple ditches of circuit Z that

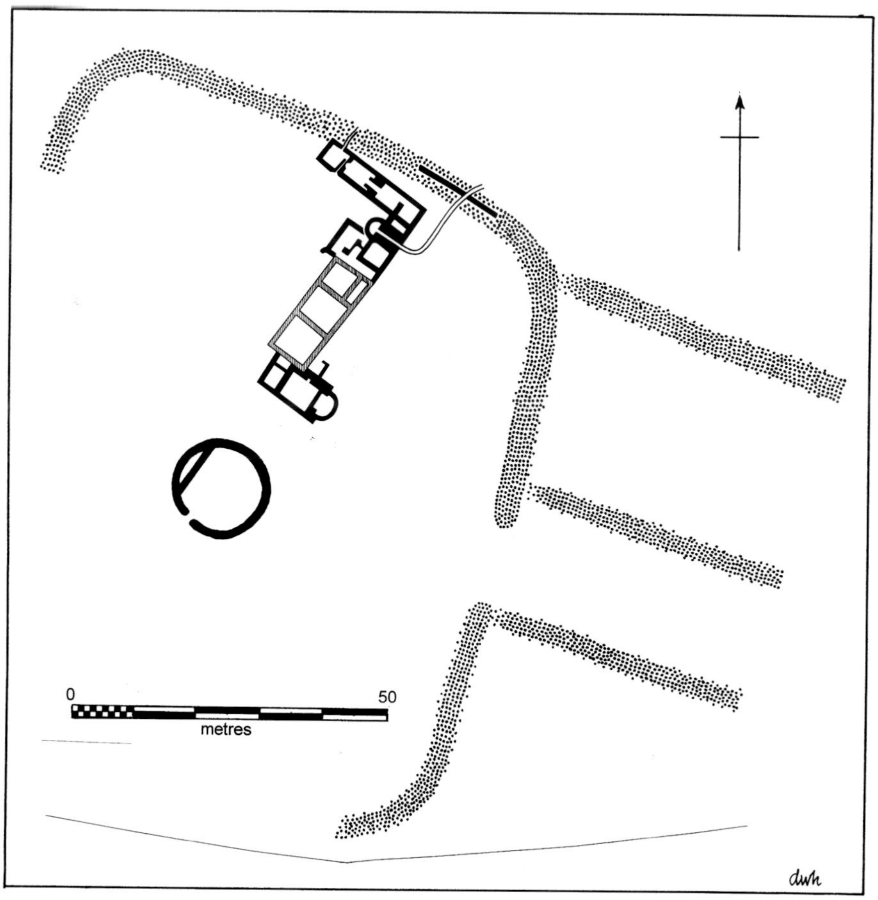

Figure 14: Holme House, Piercebridge, enclosure with annexe: sketch plan based on air photographs by Professor J. K. St Joseph, and excavation.

Figure 15: Ingleby Barwick, Stockton-on-Tees, enclosure.

Figure 16: Piercebridge Roman bridge piers and abutment.

encompass the hillfort on its east side, and, less plausibly, the outer linear earthworks W, X and Y that are hardly focused on the hillfort at all, and are in all probability earlier. Richmond and St Joseph (1982) stressed the difference in construction between these works and the hillfort ramparts, and were in no doubt, even in the absence of any definitive structural or material associations, that these were all Roman military works. The fact that their layout was less than optimal for military effectiveness in relation to the hillfort was attributed to the fact that they were for training rather than for investing the occupied hillfort. The weakness of the case, apart from the lack of dating evidence, is the absence of any definitive structures that could be regarded as Roman and military. Halliday (1982) on the other hand provided an alternative context for these various outworks in the various examples known in the Borders of hillforts, where the surrounding landscape included linear earthworks, the purpose of which was presumably stock control or the division of arable land from pasture. The most obvious of these are at White Hill and Tamshiel Rig in Roxburghshire, but, as we shall see, hillforts in the lowlands of East Lothian and Berwickshire are similarly surrounded by landscape divisions, in this case in the form of pit-alignments. An important contribution of air photography, however, has been to show the extent of cord-rigging between and around these earthworks, seemingly overlying the banks in some areas. Normally regarded as earlier Iron Age, it is possible that this form of small-scale agriculture continued much later.

In the case of Burnswark (Fig. 17a) the hill-fort was certainly occupied in the earlier Iron Age, but its later use is

Figure 17a: Burnswark, Dumfriesshire, native hillfort with Roman siege-works.

Figure 17b: Burnswark, Dumfriesshire, cord-rig in south-east corner of south camp.

Figure 18: Newstead, Melrose, Roxburghshire.

less clear. The defences at the northern end of the site were not apparently maintained, but a scatter of early Roman material with roundhouses at the south-western end suggests there may have been some continuing occupation. Dating of the Roman works is still unclear, though the southern camp, with its three artillery platforms, overlies in one corner a small fortlet of presumed Antonine date. Specialist metal-detector survey of Roman sling bullets along the southern ramparts (summarized in Harding, 2017: 233-4), however, suggests that they were the product of a serious assault and not just practice, and it would certainly have been odd to have a complex siege training facility so far north of the frontier in potentially hostile territory. A further puzzle is the small patch of cord-rig agriculture on the air-photograph of the south-eastern corner of the southern camp (Fig. 17b), of which apparently no trace can be detected on the ground.

Elsewhere the siting of Roman forts was presumably based not just on strategic locations but consequentially in locations that previously had served as important regional *foci*. Newstead (Fig. 18) by Melrose in Roxburghshire is a case in point, beneath the dominating Eildon hills, where a major native centre on Eildon Hill North (Fig. 19) was traditionally regarded as the native stronghold of the Selgovae at the time of the Roman conquest. In fact, excavation in the 1980s (Rideout *et al.* 1992) has shown that there was occupation on the hill in the later Bronze Age, and again in the Roman period, but virtually no evidence for activity in the immediately pre-Roman Iron Age. At what stage the encircling ramparts were constructed is also unclear, but it seems likely that they were added at a relatively early stage. In any event, the conventional view that this was the site of a major tribal stronghold or *oppidum* on the eve of the conquest is not long tenable. The absence of tangible archaeological remains need not mean that the site was not one of periodic assembly and traditional significance to the local community, of course, but its relationship to the Roman military sites is archaeologically undemonstrated.

Hillforts, community strongholds and lesser ditched enclosures

For much of the twentieth century hillforts were regarded as the archetypal field monument of the British Iron Age. Earlier antiquaries and field archaeologists had thought of them as Bronze Age, Roman or even Danish camps, and research over the past forty years has confirmed their origins in the later Bronze Age, even if most enjoyed their main period of occupation in the Iron Age. In Northern Britain hillforts were re-used or established *de novo* in the early historic period, and in regions north of the Roman frontier especially there is no reason why they should not have been occupied or re-occupied, if intermittently, over two millennia.

In Northern Britain in general the areas enclosed and scale of construction hardly rival the major hillforts of the south, but there is still a substantial difference between some of the larger enclosed hill settlements like Eildon Hill North (Fig. 19) or Hownam Law (Pl. 11) and the smaller, defensively-located enclosures like the Castles, Morebattle (Pl. 12) that in area enclosed are scarcely more than defended villages and in some instances are hardly distinguishable from protected homesteads. Some certainly stand out as potentially important regional *foci* on account of prominent location, like Yeavering Bell in Northumberland (Pl. 13), enclosing scores of house emplacements, or Carrock Fell in Cumbria (Pl. 14), at 670m O.D. (2174 ft) showing no extant trace of permanent settlement. Most of these key sites have never been excavated.

For an older generation of archaeologists, an implicit assumption was that later prehistoric fortification was cumulative, starting with simple palisaded enclosures and progressively developing first univallate then multivallate defensive earthworks or stoneworks. This model was based upon Mrs Piggott's (1948) excavations at Hownam Rings, Roxburghshire (Pl. 10), where such a sequence concluded with a phase of undefended settlement, dating to the early Roman period, in which the houses spilled over the enclosure earthworks on their eastern flank. The earlier phases of palisaded enclosure are hardly visible on the air photograph, but may just be seen emanating from the south-west entrance (bottom left). Subsequent research, needless to say, has shown that the 'Hownam model' is not universally applicable, even in southern Scotland and the Borders, but that area enclosed and complexity of enclosure are factors determined by prevailing social or economic circumstances rather than a standard unilinear sequence. It is hard to believe that the palisaded enclosure at Blackbrough, Hownam (Pl. 15), for example, would have survived as an extant feature through the later construction and use of the surrounding hillfort. Some hillforts nevertheless evidently did begin life as palisaded or stockaded enclosures, becoming more elaborately enclosed progressively over time. We should recognize that building a timber fence or stockade was simply a technique of enclosure that could equally be used for defensive purposes and for protecting domestic and agricultural settlements of non-defensive proportions. As such, it is hardly diagnostic either culturally or chronologically, though similar usage may characterize particular regions or periods. In fact, some larger palisaded sites were tantamount to hillforts without the rubble infilling or backing of their timber stockades. The enclosed area at Stanshiel Hill, Hownam (Pl. 16), is certainly of hill-fort proportions, but appears never to have acquired earthworks. Thowliestane Hill, Hownam (Pl. 17), and Craik Moor, Morebattle (Pl. 18), both have double lines of palisading, which, had they been cross-braced and infilled with rubble, would have made a classic timber-framed rampart. Hayhope Knowe, Morebattle (Pl. 24), initially was enclosed by a double palisade, and did subsequently acquire embankments around its eastern circuit at least.

Part of the problem lies in dating the defensive earthworks that characteristically enclose these sites. Prominent hill-tops may well have been the focus of community activity from earlier prehistoric times, but dating at which stage the enclosing earthworks were added, and whether these were cumulative in their construction, requires targeted and possibly quite extensive research excavation with no guarantee of unequivocal results. A further problem is that the category of hillforts includes a great variety of field monuments, whose superficial similarities of location and construction may belie their diversity in date and function. In a class of its own is the landscape enclosure at Stanwick in north Yorkshire (Pl. 19a,b), covering an area of around 750 acres, which Wheeler's excavations in 1952-3 established included an area of intensive occupation dating to the first century AD and concentrated in the Tofts Field. His sequence of progressive enlargements, initially excluding Henah Hill, from which the defences were thereby vulnerably overlooked, but incorporating the putatively boggy Mary Wild Beck to complete its defensive circuit, was not wholly convincing. More particularly, however, Wheeler's determination to interpret Stanwick in terms of the documented history of the mid-first century AD strained the meagre archaeological evidence beyond reasonable inference. More recent fieldwork (Haselgrove, 2016) has confirmed that the site was one of considerable importance, perhaps not as the stronghold of resistance to Rome as Wheeler imagined, but benefiting from trade with Romanized centres in the south.

An issue of continuing interest is the relationship between hillforts and the surrounding landscape. Some major sites like Traprain Law are surrounded by lesser enclosed and unenclosed settlements, and whilst not all need have been in contemporary use the probability must be that a number of these were occupied as contemporary subordinates to the regional focus. The Traprain Law environs and the East Lothian plain more widely have been the subject of intensive air survey over the years (McMillan, 2001), as a result of which enclosed settlements of both rectilinear and curvilinear form have generally been assigned to the Iron Age. The Traprain Law Environs Project (Haselgrove, 2009), carried out by Durham University from 2000 to 2004, involving selective excavation, showed a more complex pattern of relationships between the hillfort and its satellites, whilst excavation at Traprain itself once

Figure 19: Eildon Hill North, Melrose, Roxburghshire, showing perimeter earthworks with house platforms on lower slopes and nearer summit.

Figure 20: Chesters, Drem, East Lothian, hillfort and adjacent enclosure.

Figure 21: Kae Heughs, Barney Mains, East Lothian, hillfort and pit-alignments.

again showed that the immediately pre-Roman Iron Age was not a period of intensive occupation. Within such a regional structure the focal site, like Traprain, evidently need not always have been occupied to the same degree, or to have fulfilled the same function or relationship to the catchment area. On the other hand, Traprain plainly was an important regional centre during the second and third centuries AD, when it is possible that some of the rectilinear enclosures identified from the air in the vicinity were still in occupation.

The hillforts at the Chesters at Drem (Fig. 20) and Kae Heughs, Barney Mains (Fig. 21), must also have functioned within a landscape context, and are surrounded by linear features, including ditches, pit-alignments or double pit-alignments that were evidently designed to divide the landscape in some meaningful way. Quite how remains a puzzle, but presumably the upcast from the pits formed a continuous if low bank that would have formed a clear boundary if not a serious barrier. There are also other smaller enclosed sites in close proximity, notably the palisaded site at Sixpence Strip and the small, rectilinear ditched enclosure on the ridge immediately north of the hillfort (Pl. 20), though field research has yet to establish whether these were in contemporaneous occupation. The Chesters itself is an enigmatic hillfort. It is often remarked that its defensive capability is compromized by its being overlooked from higher ground to the south. Yet its multivallate earthworks, especially around its entrances, are as elaborate as any hillfort's in Northern Britain.

Dating later Iron Age use or re-use of hillforts remains problematical, partly through lack of excavation, and partly because of the relative poverty and undiagnostic character of the material assemblage, so that any modern assessment would be reliant upon recovering samples for radiometric assay. The former assumption that hillforts reached their apogee on the eve of the Roman conquest is plainly erroneous, and it might be expected that those that were in occupation would have been forcibly decommissioned, but in Dumfriesshire Castle O'er (Pl. 21) and perhaps nearby Bailiehill (Pl. 22) remained in use (Mercer, 2018), perhaps indicating that the native community in the buffer zone was in a treaty relationship with the Roman military authorities. Some hillforts like Bonchester Hill in Roxburghshire and Clatchard Craig in Fife were re-occupied in the post-Roman period. Others, notably the regional centres at Dunadd in Argyll and Dundurn, Perthshire (Pl. 23), were newly established in the early historic period. One innovation, the nuclear fort, characterized by successive plateaux around a central citadel, as at Buchtrig, Hownam (Fig. 22), was first recognized by Robert Stevenson at the type-site of Dalmahoy, Midlothian. The hierarchy of descending plateaux is plainly dependent upon the natural configuration of the hill, and Rubers Law, Roxburghshire (Fig. 23) is not strictly a nuclear fort in layout, but from its extensive re-use of Roman stonework evidently was occupied in the post-Roman period. Leslie Alcock's exploratory excavations of a series of key sites in the 1980s demonstrated that for the most part they were innovations of the post-Roman period, which may well reflect significant changes in the social structure and use of hillforts in the later Iron Age. There remains nevertheless a good deal of variety in hillfort layout and design, and in many instances, like Dun Nosebridge on Islay (Fig. 24), the date of construction and occupation is quite unknown. The rectangular outline of its innermost enclosure has prompted comparison with oblong forts, though there is no evidence of vitrification at Dun Nosebridge, and from its complexity one might suspect late use or re-use of the site.

Among smaller hillforts of the earlier Iron Age one of the most striking, the Chesters at Spott in East Lothian (Pl. 26) has multivallate defences that almost certainly reflect multi-period construction, with a complexity of entrances and apparently surviving internal houses. It is broadly similar in size and layout to its excavated neighbour at Broxmouth, near Dunbar (Armit and McKenzie, 2013), which was obliterated by development in the late 1970s, and which was certainly occupied through the second half of the first millennium BC. Though the state of preservation cannot always be judged from air photographs, it would surely warrant excavation under controlled research conditions. Some small hillforts were unquestionably occupied as defended villages of closely-packed roundhouses, like the excavated settlement at Hayhope Knowe, Morebattle (Pl. 24; Piggott, 1949), occupied in the early Iron Age, first as a palisaded enclosure, then with earthworks enhancing its slightly enlarged perimeter. The houses are seemingly aligned in an orderly layout facing a central street running between opposed entrances. On the slopes outside the settlement there are traces of cord-rig agriculture, but oddly there are also patches of cord-rigging just inside, over the earlier palisade and apparently lapping up to the earthworks on the northern side. Camp Tops (Pl. 25) also has cord-rigging outside the hillfort. Here too there is a suggestion that the interior was divided by a street running between entrances at opposite ends, though the pattern of ring-ditch houses is not quite so clear as its near neighbour's. At Sundhope Kipp, Hownam (Pl. 27), the densely-packed settlement is especially formidably defended at its less precipitous northern end, while the entrance on the east side is approached by a narrow defile between the ends of the multivallate defences and the steep hill-slope. With just the single entrance, there is here no obvious evidence for a planned layout of the houses in the interior.

Other enclosures, identified as crop-marks in lowland contexts in south-eastern Scotland, though protected by double or multiple earthworks, show little evidence of internal occupation. The twin enclosures at Ayton in Berwickshire (Fig. 25), located defensively on the edge of a scarp without obvious entrances, are scarcely large enough

Figure 22: Moat Knowe, Buchtrig, Hownam, Roxburghshire.

Figure 23: Rubers Law, Roxburghshire.

Figure 24: Dun Nosebridge, Islay.

in area to have served more than an extended family unit, and at such close proximity must represent a related social unit, suggesting the priority of social factors over defensive efficiency. It is unfortunate that agricultural patterns obscure the ditches at their edges, since the absence of any apparent entrance causeway to either enclosure suggests that access was deliberately camouflaged or diverted. There is no evidence in the Iron Age for any form of removable bridging of ditches, and this in any case would have required the banks to have been interrupted, which might well have shown up on air photographs.

The pair of enclosures at Minto in Roxburghshire (Fig. 26) likewise are in close relationship, but have less substantial defences. The triple ditches of Brae Heads, East Linton, East Lothian (Fig. 27) evidently represented a complex succession of enclosures from the later Bronze Age through the Iron Age (Haselgrove, 2009: 109-115), including a palisaded phase not visible on the air photograph. Other ditched enclosures are low-lying like Grinsdale by the Eden in Cumbria (Fig. 28), or Springhill, Berwickshire (Pl. 28) on the banks of the Tweed. Some double enclosures like Bemersyde Moss in Berwickshire (Pl. 29) could have been designed as such; others were plainly composite, like the multiple enclosure at Howtel (Fig. 29) in Northumberland. The division between fort and protected homestead is therefore a flexible one, and even the presumption that the one served a larger community, the other at most an extended family unit, may be compromised by the evidence.

The site at Flodden, Northumberland (Fig. 30) raises the possibility that another variant of ditched enclosure may be represented, the ring-work, a term applied to a number of anomalous enclosures in eastern England of a type known from Mucking in Essex to Thwing in Yorkshire. Some years ago Anthony Harding (1987: 210, No. 124) tentatively identified the innermost ditch at Flodden as a Neolithic henge, which had been enlarged and modified in the later prehistoric period. The site is plainly multi-period, and elaborately enclosed in relation to the minimal area contained, so that the comparison with the re-use of an earlier ritual site at Thwing could be instructive. The

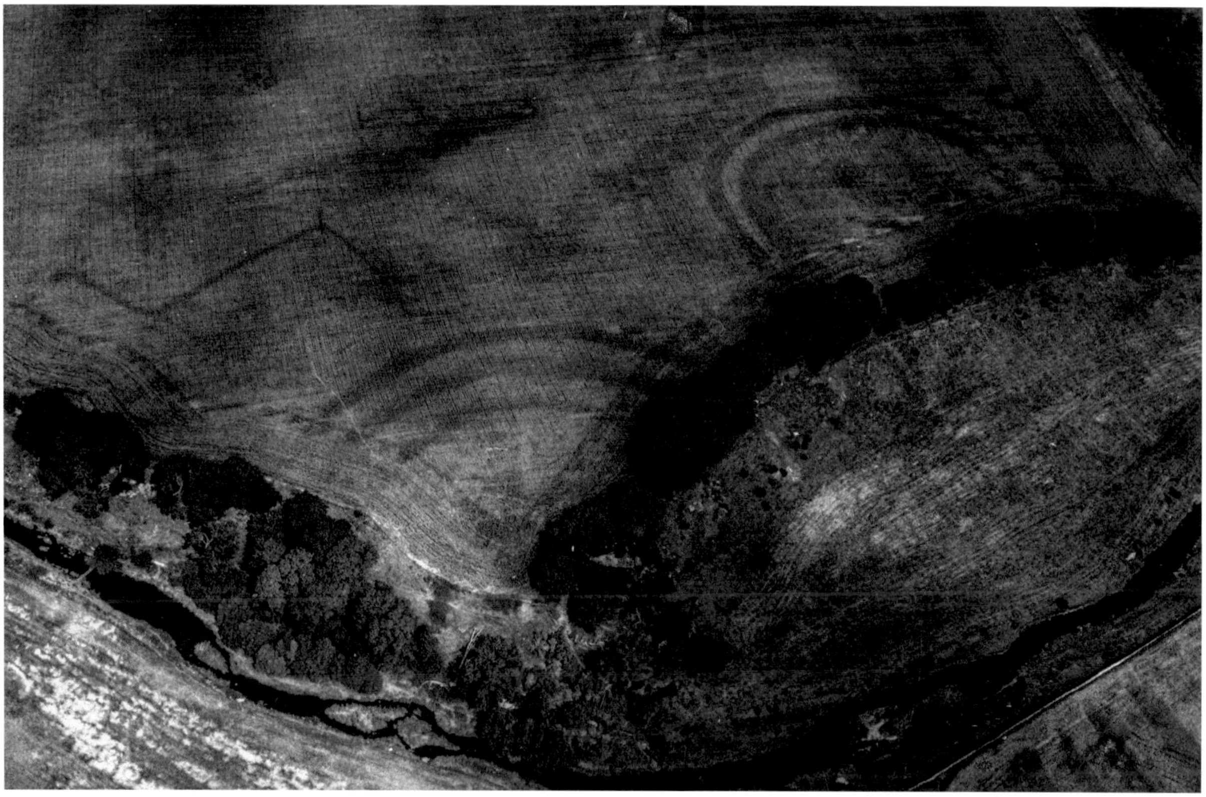

Figure 25: Ayton, Berwickshire, small, multiple-ditched enclosures.

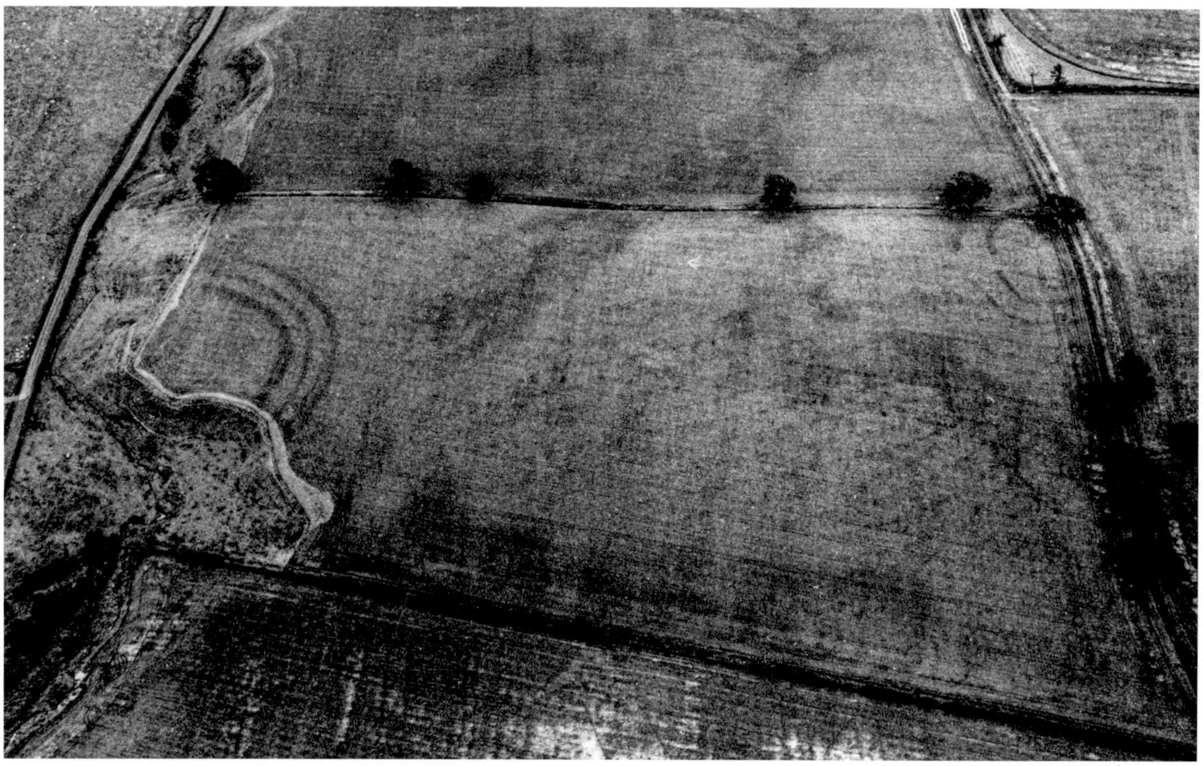

Figure 26: Minto, Roxburghshire, small, multiple-ditched enclosures.

Figure 27: Brae Heads, East Linton, East Lothian, triple-ditched enclosure.

Figure 28: Grinsdale, Cumbria, double-ditched enclosure.

Figure 29: Howtel, Northumberland, multiple-ditched enclosure.

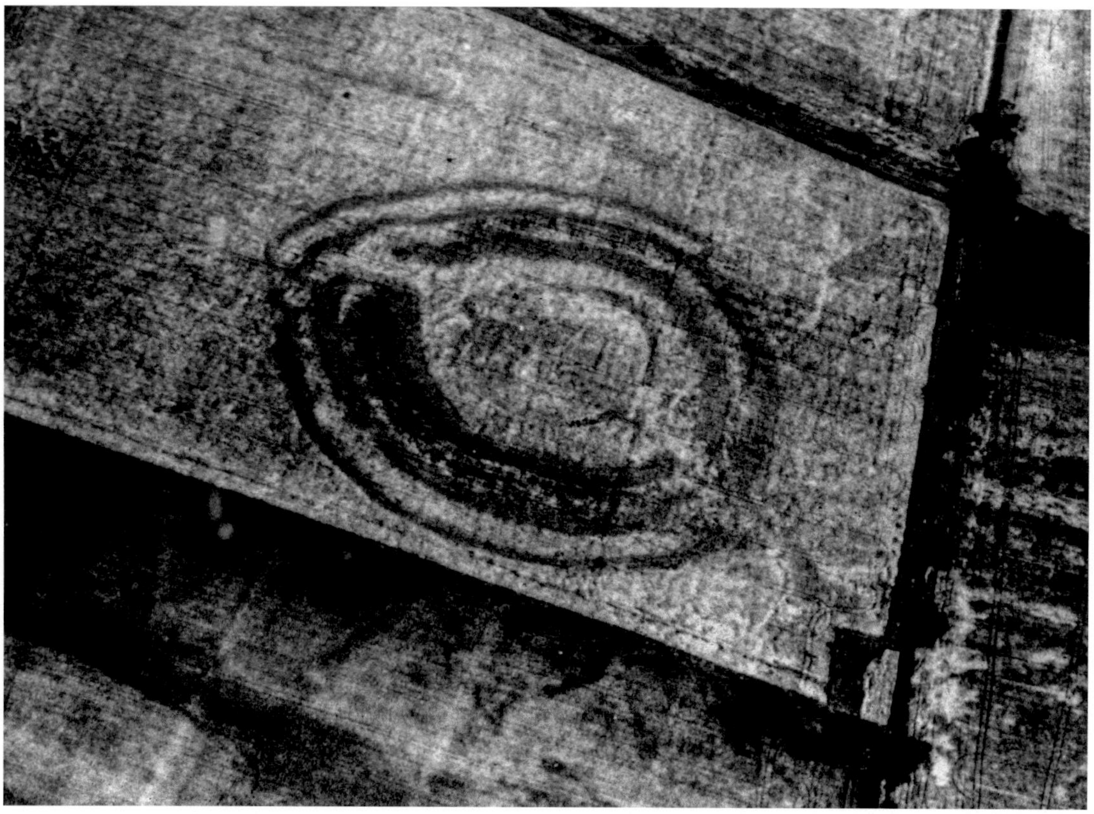

Figure 30: Flodden, Northumberland, multiple-ditched enclosure.

Milfield plain was evidently special from the Neolithic, and by the earlier and later Iron Age had acquired political and even royal status in the hillfort at Yeavering Bell and the site of *ad Gefrin* at Yeavering.

Farmsteads and protected settlements

A fundamental distinction can be drawn in classifying later prehistoric settlement between *enclosed* and *unenclosed* sites, though the presence of enclosure need not mean that the settlement did not extend beyond its boundaries. Archaeologically unenclosed settlement is much more difficult to locate, for the obvious reason that upstanding physical remains are slight compared to enclosed sites and leave minimal trace for ground or air survey to detect. Ditched enclosure therefore has been the invariable key to aerial detection, and in consequence the original number and significance of open settlements has almost certainly been greatly underestimated. In the lowlands of southern and eastern Scotland, salvage excavation in advance of development, where sites are uncovered by chance, has begun to remedy this imbalance. Open settlements certainly survive in the uplands of the Borders and in eastern Scotland, where afforestation has not obliterated earlier landscapes and where stock farming has been non-intrusive, but ring-ditch houses like those at Stirkfield in Peeblesshire (Fig. 31) are easily mis-interpreted as burial sites (RCAHMS, 1967, No. 60), and even in the uplands enclosed settlements predominate. One example where a cluster of unenclosed ring-ditch houses survives is on Hangingshaw Hill in Roxburghshire (Fig. 32), where ground survey has confirmed the presence in close proximity to the settlement of areas of cord-rig agriculture.

The concept and purpose of enclosure is fundamental to human settlement. Whether for protection against marauders or predators, or simply to define group territory, demarcating space is a basic social instinct, from the man-made stockade around a homestead to the use of natural boundaries like rivers and hill ranges to mirror tribal frontiers. The presence of double or triple ditches or palisades, assuming them to be part of a contemporary system of enclosure, rather than successive, resulting for example from a need to expand the enclosed area over time, may be regarded as socially significant, conferring status on the occupants.

Internal features of protected settlements include a variety of house types in common with those that characterize some of the hillforts. Timber construction is the dominant feature in the Borders and eastern lowlands, with some variants using stone foundations, notably the 'Votadinian' tradition of the later pre-Roman Iron Age, but not excluding some much earlier roundhouses, like those of the Tees valley later Bronze Age settlements. Posts may

Figure 31: Stirkfield, Peeblesshire, unenclosed ring-ditch houses.

be in individual post-holes, or bedded in a continuous foundation trench or 'ring-groove'. A distinctive type in south-east Scotland is the 'ring-ditch' house, so described because of its incorporation of an intermittent, shallow ditch *within* its perimeter, creating the effect of a horse-shoe shape with raised central dais, and well exemplified at Stirkfield. The purpose of the ditch remains an issue of debate, but excavation has shown that the ring-ditch lies within the perimeter wall, rather than serving as an external drip-gully.

Classic examples of the type are the pair of ring-ditch houses from High Knowes A, Alnham, Northumberland (Fig. 33; Pl. 30), where two large ring-ditch houses are each accompanied by a smaller house of ring-groove construction in a manner that suggests that these constituted a functional unit. Jobey's excavation (Jobey and Tait, 1966) also showed clearly that the ring-ditches were within the outer wall-line of the house, here defined by a ring-groove, a factor that at Braidwood, Midlothian, had previously been in doubt. It is often assumed that the larger building must have been the dwelling house, while the smaller served as an ancillary agricultural building, whereas comparison with Medieval farm complexes might well argue for the largest building having been the barn. In fact, in all probability the larger ring-ditch houses served as byre-houses, accommodating stock on the ground floor and human residents above. These principal houses are around fifteen metres in diameter, certainly allowing the possibility of an upper floor or mezzanine. Some more recently excavated examples are more than fifteen metres in diameter, not primitive 'huts' by any definition, but substantial houses requiring very considerable quantities of timber and thatch and possibly stone in terms of building materials, with implications in terms of woodland management and the social control of resources. As to dating, in north-east Scotland ring-ditch houses have now been shown to date from the mid-second millennium BC, with examples radiocarbon dated to the Middle Bronze Age from Kintore, Aberdeenshire (Cook and Dunbar, 2008). Their regular association in the Borders with cord-rig agriculture, only marginally viable by the early Iron

Figure 32: Hangingshaw Hill, Roxburghshire, unenclosed ring-ditch houses and cord-rig agriculture.

Figure 33: High Knowes A, Alnham, Northumberland, palisaded settlement with ring-ditch and ring-groove houses.

Age, might well suggest that here too the ring-ditch house had earlier origins, though we should not assume that regionally or over time they necessarily served the same function.

We have already noted that the borderline between small fort and protected homestead is a largely semantic one. Enclosing a site with ditch or palisade is a constructional technique that need not define function or social role; both may be used around homesteads and stock compounds or around larger protected settlements. A distinction may be drawn, however, from the character of the settlement enclosed, whether socially it might be regarded as the homestead of a single, nuclear family or a small village of several families within a kin group. High Knowes B, one hundred metres to the east of High Knowes A (Pl. 30), and seemingly in broadly contemporaneous occupation, was also enclosed by a double palisade, but in this instance contained a compact layout of both ring-ditch and ring-groove houses, none of them intersecting in a manner that might have suggested multi-period construction. The proximity of two palisaded enclosures of such disparate internal occupation raises fundamental issues about the social organization of the local Iron Age communities.

Figure 34: Dod Law, Northumberland, rock carvings.

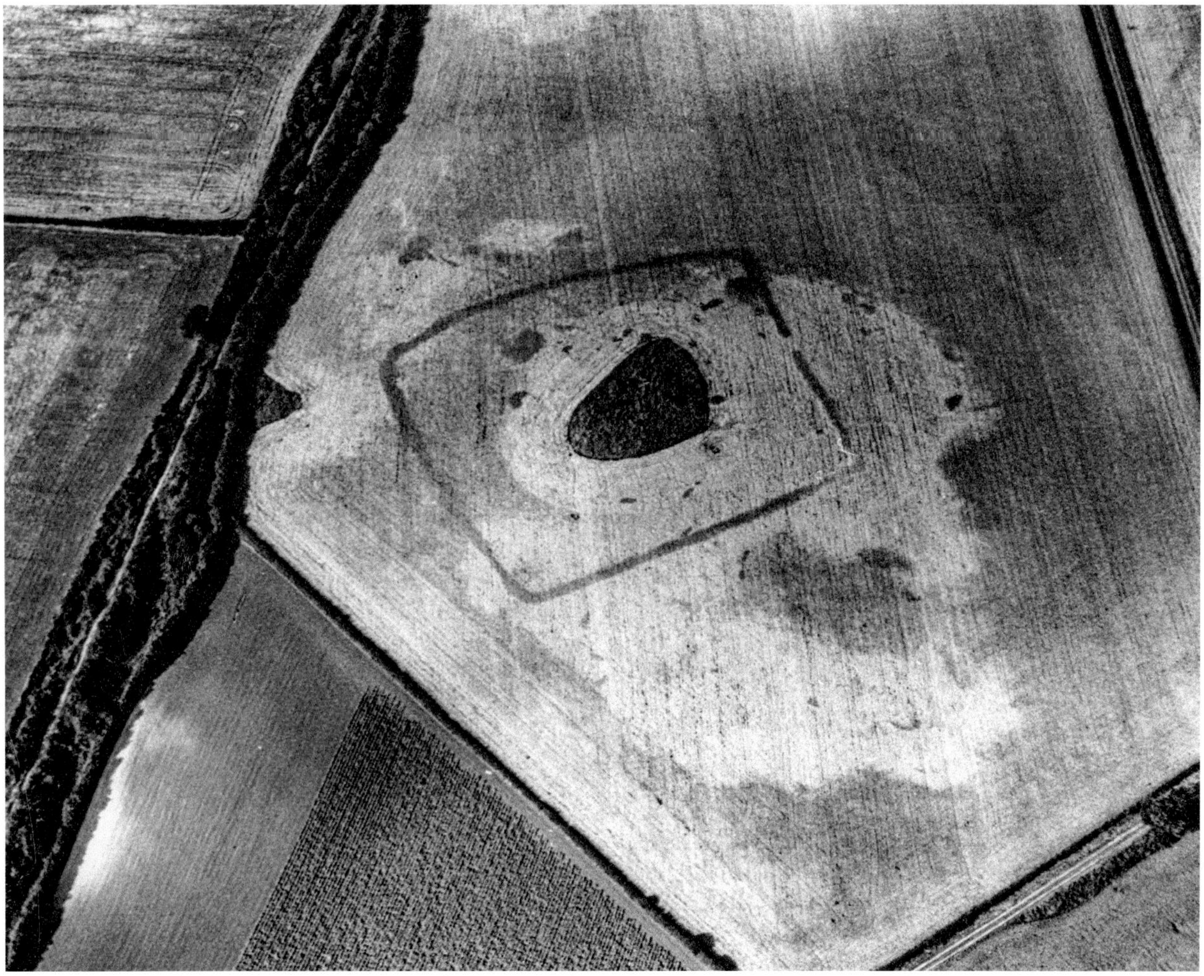

Figure 35: Dene House Farm, Thornley, Co. Durham.

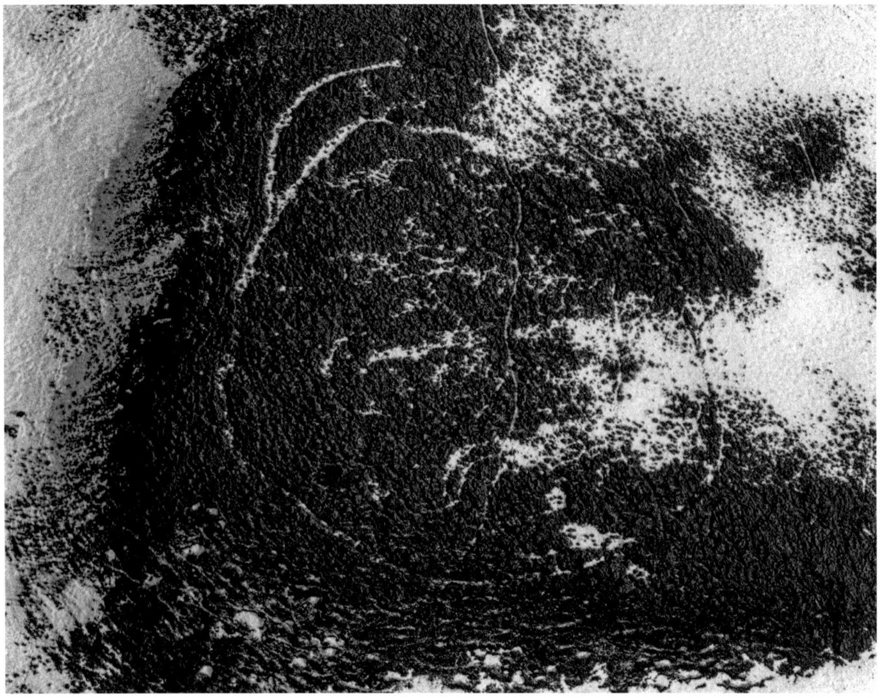

Figure 36: Fasset Hill, Morebattle, Roxburghshire.

In the light of this, it is intriguing that one of the principal rock carvings in the series at Dod Law in Northumberland (Fig. 34) features a number of circular cup marks within a triple-grooved sub-rectangular framework that bears an uncanny resemblance to the layout of a multiple-ditched or palisaded settlement like High Knowes B. This impression is enhanced by the apparent entrance into the enclosure at the base of the carving.

Larger communal groups are not restricted to palisaded settlements. We have already noted small hillforts like Camp Tops, Morebattle (Pl. 25), where the extant remains of roundhouses, even if not all in contemporary occupation, are sufficiently densely ordered that they must represent several families, whilst Sundhope Kipp, Hownam, (Pl. 27), where the surviving defences are more variable in strength around different sectors of the perimeter, must still qualify as a protected village. These communal sites stand in marked contrast to those protected homesteads, whether rectilinear or curvilinear in external plan, that contain just a single principal roundhouse, or pair of roundhouses, sometimes with a lesser ancillary building, like those at Meldon Burn or Gray Coat in Peeblesshire. The earlier palisaded enclosure with ring-ditch houses at Pudding Law, Morebattle, Roxburghshire (Pl. 31), with its accompanying plots of cord-rig agriculture, photographed in conjunction with Roger Mercer's 1985 field survey in the Bowmont valley, probably began its early Iron Age occupation as a homestead of this kind. The counterpart south of the border is the sub-rectangular enclosure of the kind excavated by Jobey at West Brandon in Co. Durham and Burradon in Northumberland. The very distinct crop-mark enclosures at Dene House Farm, Thornley (Fig. 35), Broomside (Pl. 33) and Brandon (Pl. 34), Co. Durham, and the soil- mark at Ovingham on the north bank of the Tyne (Pl. 5) were almost certainly of this kind, though the central houses are not visible in these air photographs. In Northumberland, the Borders and southern Scotland other variants include a range of sub-circular enclosures, the significance of which in contrast to the sub-rectangular form is not clear. Rectangularity certainly need not imply Roman influence, but dating without excavation is problematical, and even then, in the past, in the absence of radiocarbon sampling, was inhibited by the poverty of the associated material assemblages.

Among smaller palisaded enclosures we have already argued that the Blackbrough palisade (Pl. 15) must be later than the hillfort, since otherwise its fugitive traces would hardly have survived. At its near neighbour Greenbrough (Pl. 32) a small, sub-rectangular compound was sufficient for its main house and secondary building (below, right) in the same paired arrangement that characterized High Knowes A. It is an astonishing reflection on how minimal has been the impact of subsequent land use that the position of the gateposts of this enclosure should still be visible. The palisaded site at Fasset Hill, Morebattle (Fig. 36), is of interest because of the outwork or forecourt shielding its entrance, while several arced snow-marks indicate the positions of internal roundhouses.

The palisaded sites at Marleyknowe, Northumberland (Fig. 37) and Gibbs Hill, Dumfriesshire (Fig. 38), by contrast, were villages of roundhouses, where the lines of enclosure were evidently rebuilt on successive occasions.

Figure 37: Marleyknowe, Northumberland, multiple palisaded enclosures with roundhouses.

Figure 38: Gibbs Hill, Dumfriesshire, multi-phased palisaded settlement with cord-rig.

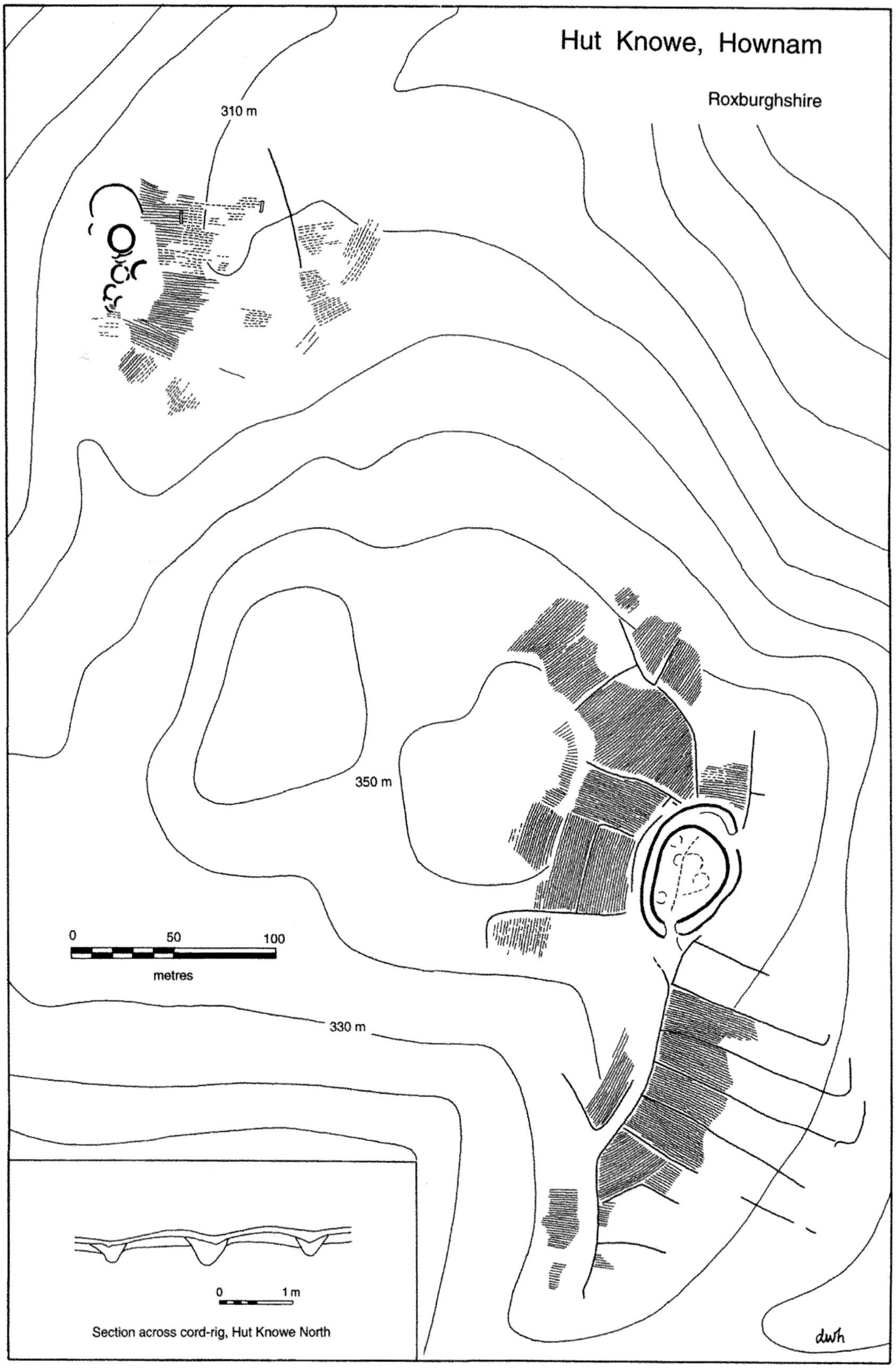

Figure 39a: Hut Knowe, Hownam, plan of principal features.

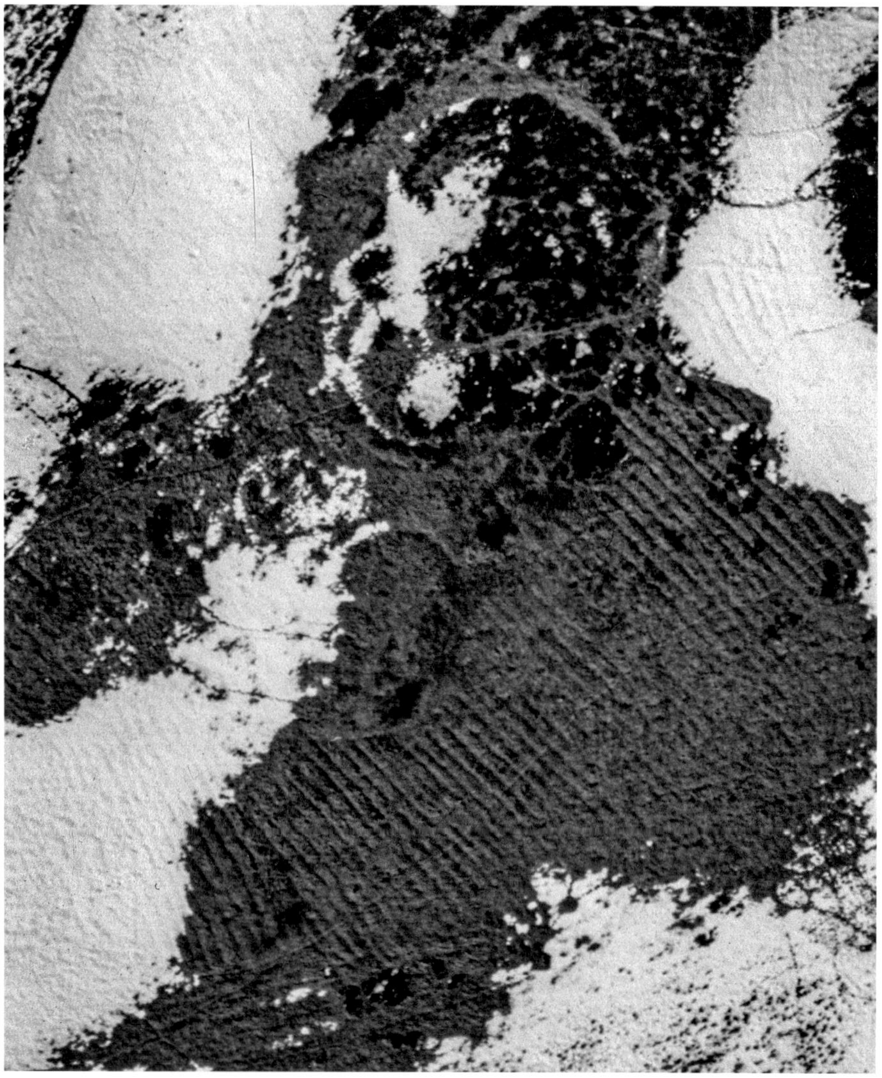

Figure 39b: Hut Knowe North, Hownam, Roxburghshire, palisaded enclosure, ring-ditch houses and cord-rig agriculture under snow.

Gibbs Hill is also notable for being encompassed by cord-rig agriculture, the fugitive character of which has been remarked earlier.

A more formal arrangement, in which some, though not all, of the cord-rig is enclosed by fields, is that at Hut Knowe, Hownam, where a small hillfort is approached by a trackway that leads through the enclosed fields (Fig. 39,a; Pl. 8). To the north the cord-rig is unenclosed, and again emanates from around a small palisaded settlement with ring-ditch houses (Fig. 39,b). The impression is of cumulative development over a protracted period of time, in which the hillfort, which itself was subject to at least one episode of reconstruction, with the enclosed fields, may have been just the latest phase. In the north settlement, too, more than one phase of activity may be represented. The palisaded enclosure is relatively small, appropriate to a single, original house, whereas the cluster of surviving ring-ditches appears to have expanded over its probable original southern limit.

One of the best examples in the Borders is the palisaded enclosure at Woden Law East (Fig. 40), where swathes of cord-rig extend up to the palisade trench on all sides, but significantly do not intrude upon the settlement, suggesting that it was indeed part of the contemporary landscape. Within the enclosure at least two houses are visible as arcs in the snow, with possible indications of others.

We have already noted major examples of landscape division in the linear ditches and pit-alignments around the hillforts at Drem in East Lothian. This form of landscape division is known from the Neolithic, though dating the pits in the absence of artefact associations or material for radiocarbon sampling can be problematical, and it is by no means limited to contexts in which hillforts are focal. The most concentrated group of putatively later prehistoric pit-alignments was well known from the 1950s from air photography around Castlesteads at Whitecraig, (Figs 41a,b; Pl. 35), where four pit-alignments, one of them double, run parallel to each other at a distance of 300-400 metres,

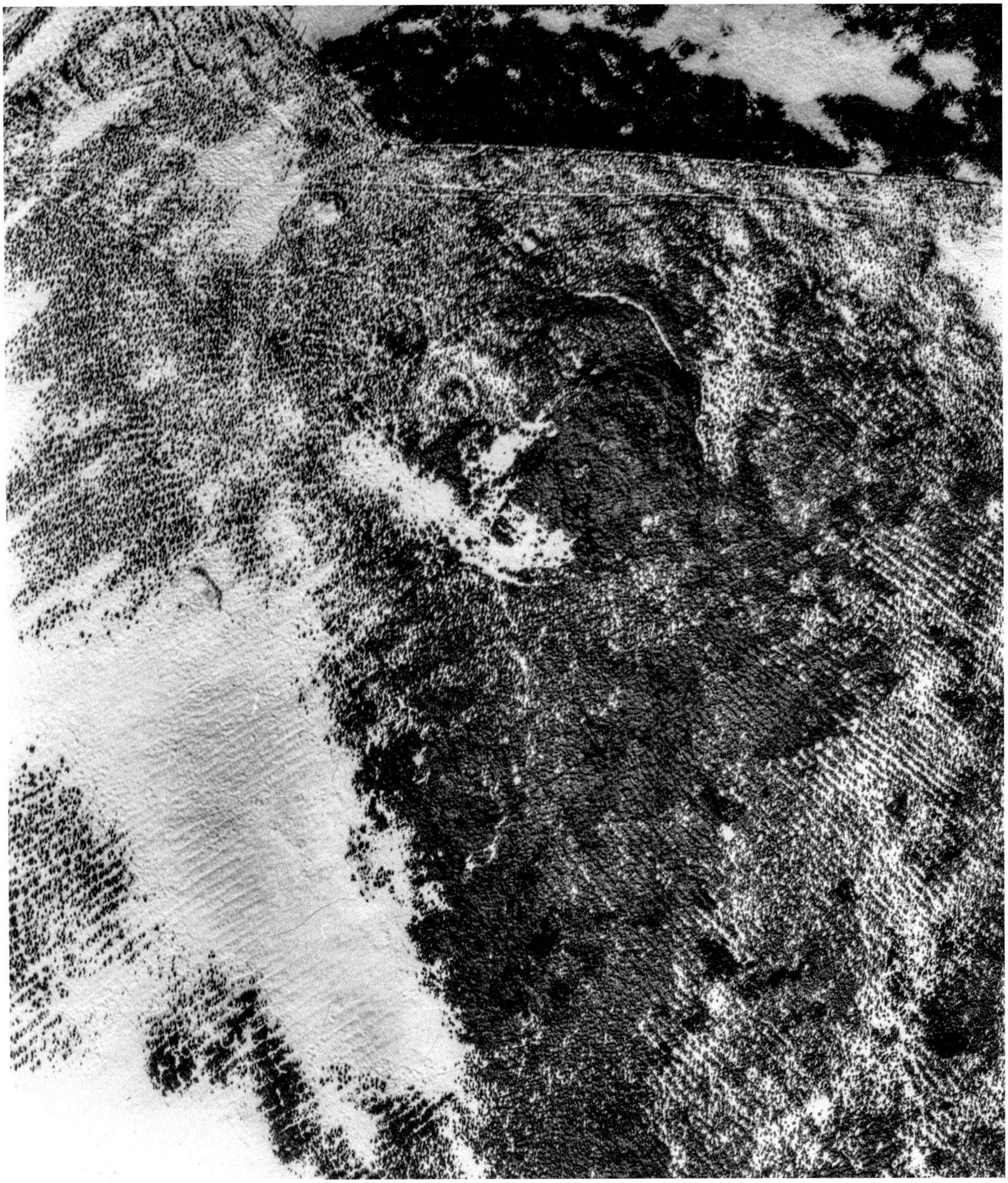

Figure 40: Woden Law East, Hownam, Roxburghshire, palisaded enclosure with ring-ditch houses and cord-rig agriculture under snow.

forming blocs of land up to 24 ha in extent (Halliday, 1982, Fig. 1; Harding, 2017, Fig. 3.17). Sample excavation of pits and enclosures was undertaken by Professor Stuart Piggott and R. J. C. Atkinson with the Edinburgh University Archaeological Society in the 1950s (*Proceedings of the Prehistoric Society*, 24, 1957: 219), but the results were never published, and the pit-alignments have now been partly obliterated by the Edinburgh southern by-pass. A subsequent radiocarbon date for one of the pits, however, indicated possible construction in the first century BC. The circular palisade west of the pit-alignment appears to contain a concentric circular building; the rectilinear

Figure 41a: Whitecraig, East Lothian, pit-alignment and enclosures.

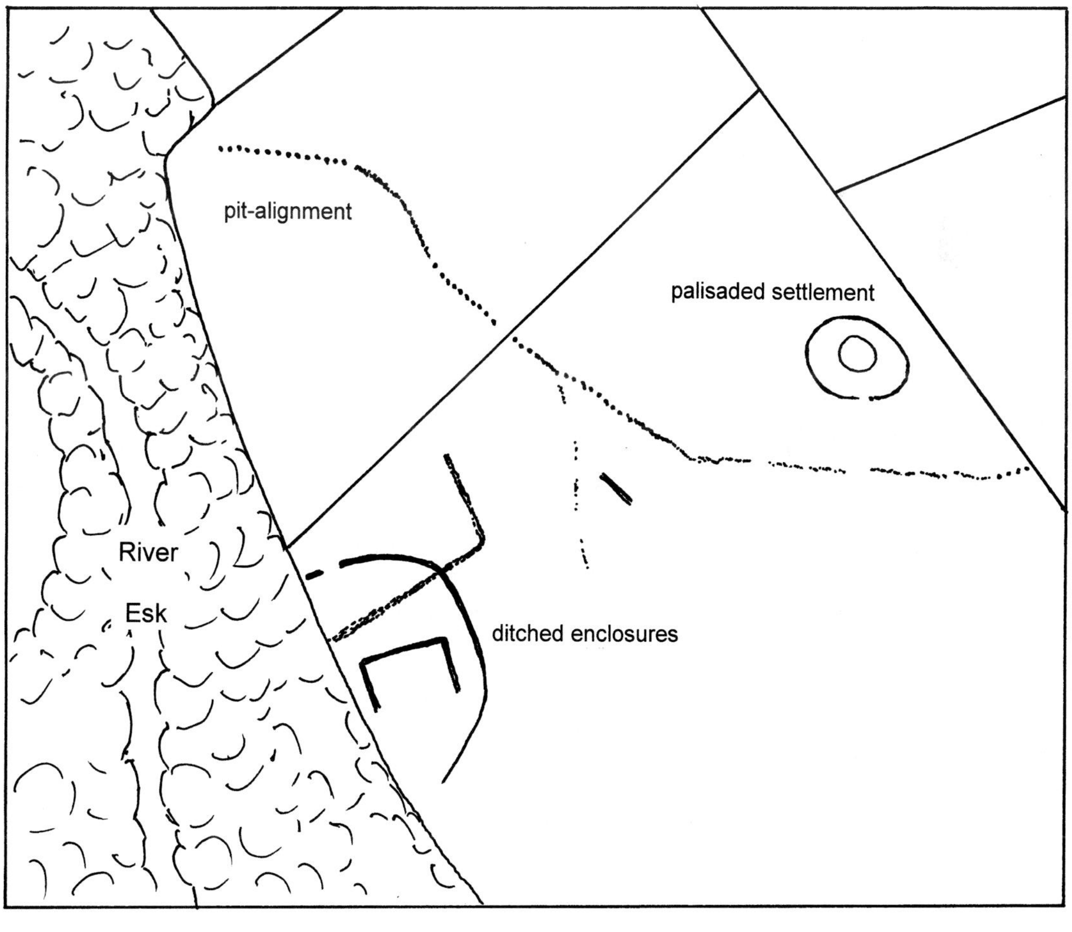

Figure 41b: Whitecraig, East Lothian, sketch plan of principal features.

Figure 42: Marygold Plantation, Berwickshire, pit-alignment.

ditched feature and larger ditched enclosure to the east under the edge of the wood may represent different phases of construction. To the west is the parallel double pit-alignment (Pl. 35b) with adjacent palisaded enclosure, and beyond that were at least two more parallel alignments.

The relationship between pit-alignment and ditched enclosure at Whitelaw Hill, East Lothian (Pl. 36) is not clearly established. It appears to stop short of the enclosure, at a point where the latter has several gaps in its ditch. Indeed, the appearance of at least five gaps, presumably indicating entrances, is itself unusual for an Iron Age enclosure, though not without parallel. Quite how pit-alignments functioned in contrast to a continuous linear ditch remains unclear, but they are a landscape feature from the Neolithic to early historic periods, with examples occasionally surviving extant until recent times, as at Marygold Plantation in Berwickshire (Fig. 42).

Pit-alignments are also in evidence near the Eye Water at Ayton in Berwickshire (Fig. 43a,b), in proximity to a twin palisaded enclosure that has a more regularly circular outline than most Iron Age palisaded homesteads, with the possible exception of Sixpence Strip at Drem. There are in addition several ring-ditches adjacent to the pit-alignment and in the near field that could be either houses or possibly burials, though Iron Age burials in East Lothian and Berwickshire tend to be cist-graves or variants rather than ring-ditch barrows. In the main field these features are showing late in the season as reversal marks, bleached out against the neutral background.

Native settlements of the Roman period in northern England and southern Scotland commonly employed more stone construction than their predecessors, though the 'Votadinian' tradition of stone houses was already introduced before the conquest. The Tyne-Forth region in particular has been a focus of research over many years, notably associated with the fieldwork of Professor George Jobey, who from the 1960s established the Romano-British occupation of a number of distinctive settlement types, ranging from individual homesteads to larger clusters of houses that warrant description as villages. In some cases these settlements occupied or overlay earlier sites, including hillforts that had evidently been decommissioned, as at Greaves Ash, Linhope, Northumberland (Fig. 44), where the Romano-British settlement spills over earthwork defences of the Iron Age hillfort. At the same time a separate settlement was established to the south-west, with a network of trackways and field boundaries between. These village settlements stand in contrast to homesteads, notably those of North Tynedale with their rectilinear stone-walled enclosures, and others of oval or curvilinear plan, where up to half a dozen stone-built houses fronted a communal yard, which presumably accommodated an extended family or kin group. In Redesdale, these settlements are associated with areas of cord-rig, suggesting that this

Figure 43a: Eye Water, Ayton, Berwickshire, enclosure, pit-alignment and ring-ditches.

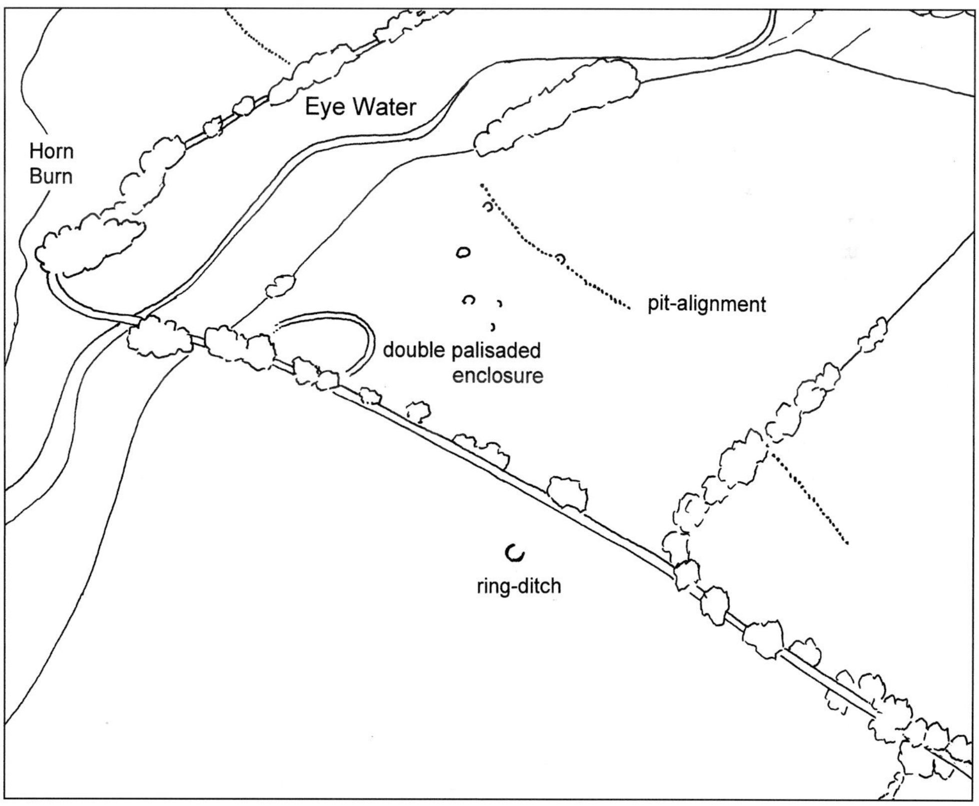

Figure 43b: Eye Water, Ayton, Berwickshire, sketch plan of principal features.

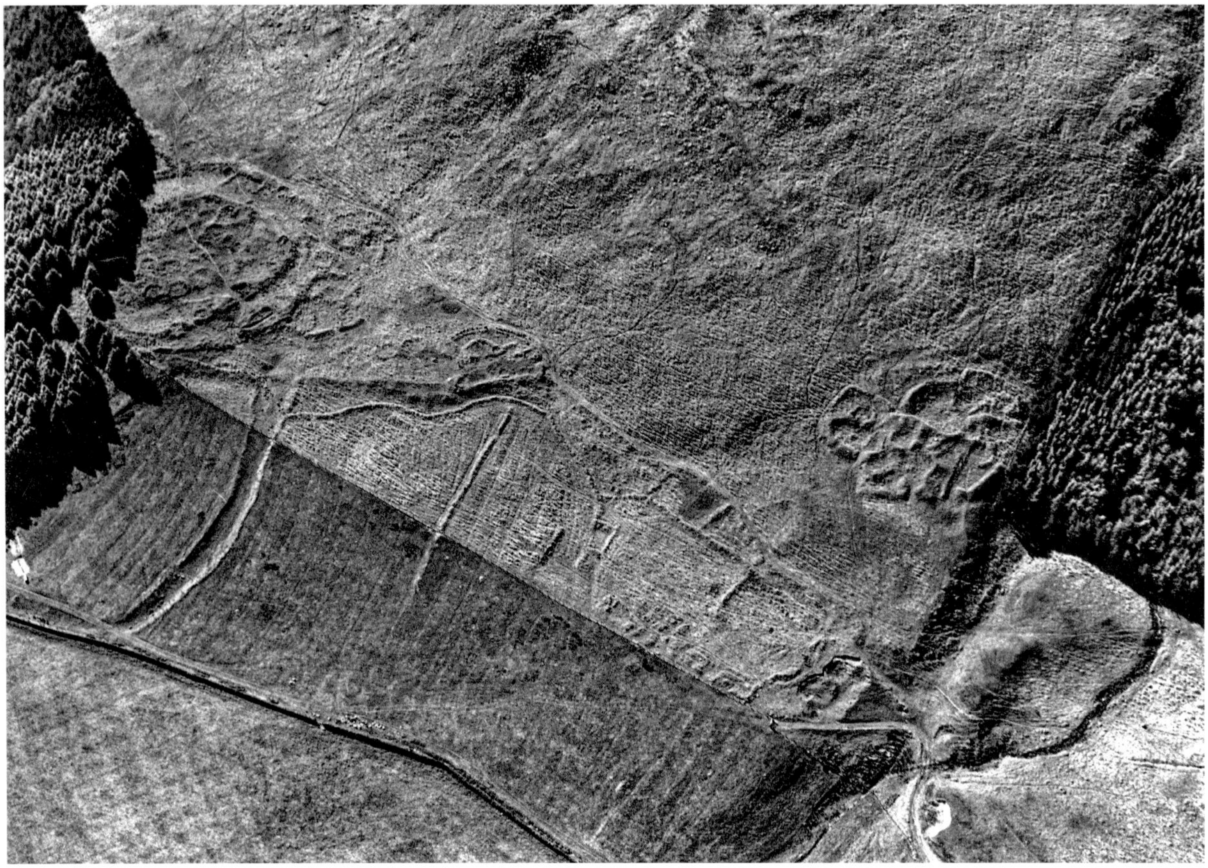

Figure 44: Greaves Ash, Northumberland, hillfort and native settlements.

Figure 45: Haystack Hill, Northumberland, native settlement with Medieval rig-and-furrow.

form of cultivation was still practised in the Romano-British period.

At Haystack Hill (Fig. 45) in the Breamish Valley separate sub-circular and sub-rectangular enclosures contain amorphous agglomerations of houses and ancillary buildings that evidently formed a focus for later agricultural patterns. Limited excavation in this area has shown that the Romano-British settlements may overlie much earlier occupation, dating even from the Bronze Age.

Crannogs of central Scotland

Air photography of inland lochs is a major tool in Scotland for the discovery of one of the most important and under-researched categories of field monument, namely crannogs. Crannogs are artificial or reinforced natural islands, generally assumed to have served as settlement sites- 'lake-dwellings' or 'lakeside dwellings'- dating mostly from later prehistoric to early historic times. Some may have been built as early as the Neolithic, and others were certainly re-used as late as the sixteenth and seventeenth centuries. As a rule of thumb we might infer that the best-preserved and most upstanding, like Eilean Breaban (Pl. 37) or perhaps Mary's Distaff (Pl. 38) in Loch Tay, were the latest occupied, whilst the more fugitive remains might prove to be earlier. Radiocarbon dating is increasingly indicating that the majority was built and used in the later prehistoric or early historic periods, broadly between 500 BC and AD 500 (Dixon, 2007), and as such they should be treated alongside other contemporary forms of Iron Age settlement. It is ironic that the central Highlands, where the densest distribution of crannogs is found, was represented on Piggott's (1966) map of Scottish Iron Age provinces as virtually a barren landscape, where all the more heavily-populated provinces had their common boundaries. In reality, the distribution of crannogs is tantamount to an extra province, and even allowing for the fact that they span a thousand years of prehistory and early history, their numbers in Loch Tay, Loch Awe and Loch Lomond surely signify a significant exploitation of these inland waterways in the ancient past.

Within the British Isles, crannogs are virtually unknown except in Scotland. There are certainly crannogs in Ireland, though they generally take a rather different form, with some of the more celebrated sites dating from the Early Christian period rather than the earlier Iron Age. In Scotland they occur principally in the central Highlands and in the south-west (Cavers, 2010), where there are lochs suitable for their construction. A cognate class of island duns, especially in the Western Isles, show similar characteristics, but are built more substantially of stone in the monumental Atlantic roundhouse tradition.

Crannogs were recognized and studied by pioneers in underwater archaeology from the later nineteenth century, but it is only relatively recently that the full potential of these sites has been recognized, and investment in this rewarding field of study is still surprisingly limited. Though equipment and techniques may be common to all branches of underwater archaeology,conditions pertaining to the excavation of loch-side settlements in relatively shallow inland waters may differ significantly from those of maritime archaeology. Even within Scotland, circumstances may differ radically, excavation in mainland, deep-water lochs like Loch Tay or Loch Awe presenting quite different problems from the inland lochs of the Western Isles, where deep silts and unpredictable weather limit underwater visibility. In the mainland deep-water lochs crannogs are commonly located on a relatively shallow shelf, sometimes quite close to the shore, like Craggan in Loch Tay (Pl. 39), which must have risked exposure in drier summers, sometimes further distant, as at Milton Morenish in Loch Tay (Pl. 43) or Bandry in Loch Lomond (Pl. 41), just short of where the loch profile plunges to greater depths.

Crannogs would have served as protected homesteads for a single family unit comparable to the Iron Age homesteads of the Borders or the stone-built roundhouses of Atlantic Scotland. Though air photography and water-borne survey have detected sites like Dall Bay in Loch Tay (Pl. 40) or Cameron Bay in Loch Lomond (Pl. 42), where pairs of crannogs occur in close proximity, these sites were not necessarily in contemporary occupation, and there is no evidence in central Scotland for the existence of crannog 'villages', or of lochside clusters as has recently been found in the south-west. Though they are sometimes less than a kilometre apart, as at Oakbank and Fearnan Hotel (Pl. 44), they would not always have been inter-visible, especially when tucked into a sheltered cove like Mill Cairn in Loch Lomond (Pl. 45), though they would certainly have been visible to neighbours across the loch. Often, however, as perhaps at Strathcashel Point, Loch Lomond (Pl. 46), the siting of the crannog would have been as much for access to adjacent land on shore as for the merits of the lacustrine location.

A major difference archaeologically between crannogs and their land-based equivalents is that the waterlogged environment of crannogs provides exceptionally good organic preservation, so that a range of artefactual and environmental material survives that is absent from most settlements on land. Where a site survives part on dry land, part under water, as at Dun Bharabhat in the Western Isles (Harding and Dixon, 2000), the contrast in the surviving material assemblages from the two contexts is striking. The underwater excavation recovered wooden artefacts, basket-work, heather rope and straw bedding, which would not be expected to survive on land, while quantities of animal bone under water contrasted with a virtual absence of bone from the land excavation. Examination of underwater assemblages therefore can raise serious doubts regarding the reliability of social and economic reconstruction based exclusively upon land-based survivals.

Much debate in recent years has centred upon the construction of crannogs, whether they were free-standing 'pile dwellings' in open water or whether they were built as artificial islands or on islands artificially reinforced with timber and stone. It seems probable that both techniques were used, or a combination of structural variations depending on circumstances over the long span of use or re-use of individual sites. One obvious question when we observe crannogs under water is why they should be submerged? If they were indeed pile dwellings like the experimental reconstruction at Kenmore on Loch Tay, then plainly with abandonment and collapse the debris of the building would have sunk beneath the water. But the excavators of the Oakbank crannog, on which the reconstruction was broadly based, believed that they had uncovered occupation levels effectively *in situ*, so that the site must have subsided significantly or the loch levels must have risen significantly since antiquity. Before loch levels were subject to modern controls, seasonal rise and fall could have been in the order of several metres, so that buildings, whether on stilts or on an artificial island base would need to have been built well above flood level. Even if they were intended only for seasonal use, partial immersion and drying out would accelerate decay and demand constant maintenance and repair.

A significant constraint, and perhaps one reason for the loch-side location of settlements in the central Highlands, is the scarcity of usable agricultural land. Many years ago Ian Morrison (1985) noted a correlation between the location of crannogs and parcels of potential arable land. Where the loch profile did not permit the construction of crannogs, the contours being too sheer or the location too exposed to wind and water fetch, then a land-based dun was commonly in evidence. This idea affords an apt reminder to us that crannogs should not be studied in isolation from the rest of the archaeological landscape of which they were once part. Indeed their study demands exactly the same principles and applications as the excavation of land-based sites, though necessarily adapted to their underwater context.

As in the case of crop-mark sites, it is sometimes possible to infer a kind of stratigraphy in air photographic records. The Shader site in north Lewis is a case in point (Pl. 47a). The latest and best-preserved of the island duns is clear enough, being an upstanding monument above the water level, with a causeway surviving sufficiently well to permit access. From the air in 1984 a much fainter feature was visible among the extensive patches of algae to the west, with only minimal signs of stones breaking the surface. An optimistic observer might even imagine that some stones by the shore were the remnants of an original causeway. The existence of this second crannog or island dun was subsequently confirmed by underwater survey, which also confirmed that the loch was not the most attractive for underwater excavation on account of poor visibility among other factors, a situation that has doubtless improved since the installation of a mains sewerage system in the local township. What the algae marks had concealed, however, was a third stage in the sequence. In 1987 a further air survey was undertaken when there was no algae obstructing the picture, at which stage it became clear that the 'halo' around one side of the surviving dun was not an algae mark, but the traces of an intermediate structure which had been truncated in the construction of the latest, surviving monument (Pl. 47b). This realization plainly would be significant in any assessment of the chronology of island duns, or in the development of a research strategy to investigate this class of field monument. If the archaeologist is concerned with the origins of the type, it would be the oldest, probably the faintest feature on the air photographs, which would repay excavation, rather than the most conspicuous surviving structure, which is almost certainly the youngest in the proposed sequence.

Brochs and forts of Atlantic Scotland

Brochs and duns of Atlantic Scotland are among the most vigorously debated topics in Northern British archaeology. Their definition and classification, their origins and chronology, their function and social implications have divided archaeologists for several generations, and even with the advent of modern dating technology they still provoke controversy, basically because of the insufficiency or inadequacy of the excavated data.

Perhaps the most divisive issue has been the question of dating. From the 1960s the received wisdom was that brochs dated from the first century BC or thereabouts at earliest, flourishing for no more than three or four centuries before falling into decline and being superseded by wheelhouses and other less monumental classes of building. Excavations in the Northern and Western Isles, however, notably at Old Scatness in Shetland (Dockrill *et al.* 2010, 2015), and at Dun Bharabhat, Cnip (Harding and Dixon, 2000), and the Loch na Beirgh, Riof (Harding and Gilmour, 2000), in west Lewis, have indicated older origins, perhaps from as early as the mid-first millennium BC. Radiocarbon dates are admittedly too few at present to confirm this conclusion beyond doubt, but their accumulation will surely lengthen the conventional chronology of brochs. By way of defence, traditionalists still argue not unreasonably that the architecturally more complex broch towers were probably late in the sequence. Instead of regarding these structural types as definitive and mutually exclusive, Ian Armit devised the term 'Atlantic roundhouses' to embrace the generality of massive drystone structures and their more developed counterparts, seeing them as a spectrum of regional variants without prejudice to issues of origin and chronology. Brochs and duns (or more specifically the

Figure 46: Burrian broch, North Ronaldsay, Orkney.

Figure 47: Loch of Houlland, Northmaven, Shetland.

smaller circular or sub-circular duns of house proportions) effectively belong to a broad continuum of drystone, circular buildings, the function of which was essentially domestic, though some in construction and location may display a defensive dimension.

A second question is whether brochs represent the top of a social hierarchy, and if so, what field monuments can be adduced to represent the lower orders? The idea that wheelhouses and duns fulfilled this role hardly squares with the evidence that wheelhouses for the most part post-date the decline of brochs in their main period of use. Furthermore, in some regions like Caithness the density of brochs in close proximity, even assuming that they were not all in simultaneous occupation, suggests a scenario in which there would have been too many chiefs and no indians. From excavated brochs there is very little evidence of a hierarchy in terms of the range or quality of the material assemblage, and even metal-working, sometimes taken as evidence of social status, seems too widespread to imply exclusiveness. In Orkney some brochs like Gurness on Mainland (Pl. 48) and Midhowe on Rousay (Pl. 49) are part of an enclosed 'village', where it might be possible to regard the broch itself as the 'laird's house' with lesser orders clustered around it within the protection of the compound. It is possible that Burrian broch on North Ronaldsay (Fig. 46) also had external structures within the area defined by its enclosing ramparts. The very ephemeral structures around the Gurness broch are clearly secondary to the principal broch occupation, though it is possible that a contemporary 'village' originally lay beneath these extant structures.

In Shetland brochs are known in both loch-side and promontory contexts. At the Loch of Houlland, Northmaven (Fig. 47), the broch occupies a site not unlike Bragar in Lewis, on a natural or reinforced spit projecting into the

Figure 48: Burland broch, Lerwick, Shetland.

loch, the approach to which, like the island duns of the Western Isles, is protected by lateral walls. It is also linked by a now underwater causeway to the adjacent small island, which is itself linked by a surviving causeway to the shore, on a smaller scale not unlike the complex in the loch of Sticer in North Uist. At Burland, Lerwick (Fig. 48), the broch entrance is within a few feet of the cliff edge, which must have eroded significantly since the Iron Age occupation. Furthermore, the broch's location so close to the entrance through the multiple works that protect the neck of the promontory seems incompatible with their contemporary construction and use. Levenwick (Fig. 49) is likewise sited close to the less steep cliff edge. Both brochs have evidence of secondary occupation, at Levenwick comprising a wheelhouse within the broch shell and cellular structures outside.

Brochs are known too in western Inverness-shire and Skye, notably in Glenelg and at Dun Beag, Struanmore. In the Western Isles at Carloway in north-west Lewis the walls still stand to a height of nine metres, allowing a reasonably reliable reconstruction of the broch's superstructure to be made. Around the north and west of Lewis modern settlement has been restricted to the coastal belt by encroachment of peat bog from the interior, and nowhere

Figure 49: Levenwick, Dunrossness, Shetland.

is this clearer from the air than at Borve, where the broch has been engulfed in what resembles a lunar landscape (Pl. 51, a,b). The ground galleries of the broch are now well below modern ground level, so that, were it possible to strip the peat from the surrounding area, we might uncover an Iron Age landscape virtually intact.

In terms of architectural typology very similar, though located on an island in a small inland loch, is the broch at Bragar (Pl. 50). Like the island duns of Lewis, it is approached across a stone causeway, flanking which are lateral walls of uncertain date, but possibly part of the defensive design or simply intended to present a prestigious architectural frontage to anyone attempting to access the site. These sites certainly highlight the limitations of the older archaeological typology of field monuments, since for the most part the dilapidated state of the stonework precludes any definitive statement regarding their original structural form, while their location and environmental context is hardly diagnostic culturally or chronologically. In fact from field survey, including underwater survey, and excavation, it seems probable that artificial or reinforced natural islands in inland shallow water lochs were used for settlement in the Western Isles from the Neolithic until late Medieval times, just as the crannogs of central and south-western Scotland had a protracted if intermittent currency. Promontory sites were likewise exploited over a long period of time, and relatively few instances in the Western Isles can with any confidence be assigned an Iron Age dating. One probable candidate is the promontory site at Dun Mara, Barvas, in north Lewis (Fig. 50), where an Atlantic roundhouse is apparently protected by a double rampart on the landward side. Later buildings have been built within its ruins, and no excavation has been conducted to confirm its date or character, but its similarity to the Shetland sites considered above makes it a likely candidate for an Iron Age date. Beyond its ramparts its immediate environment has been overlain with a striking pattern of later agriculture.

Figure 50: Dun Mara, Barvas, Lewis.

Larger enclosures or forts likewise are not a regular feature of the later prehistoric or early historic landscape in the Western Isles in the way that they are in Argyll and the Inner Hebrides. In the Northern Isles they are represented, however, particularly in locations that take advantage of precipitous coastal promontories. One distinctive variant, the blockhouse or gatehouse fort, is characteristic only of Shetland, though its defensive function appears to be compromised. The key factor about the blockhouse design is that the stone façade conspicuously occupies the approach to the site, but, far from extending around the entire perimeter, did not even effectively bar access to the interior. The promontory site at the Ness of Burgi, Dunrossness (Fig. 51), and the multi-phased loch-side settlement at Clickhimin, Lerwick (Fig. 52), both demonstrate this anomaly. In the case of the former its lateral limitation was perhaps dictated by the precipitous and doubtless eroding cliff edges, but in the latter instance the blockhouse plainly was designed to stop well short of the water's edge. These sites also illustrate the contrasting character of such forts, the Ness of Burgi occupying a rocky promontory, where there is no surviving evidence of structural occupation, while Clickhimin was a loch-side settlement approached from a narrow spit of land forming a natural or reinforced causeway, where there was a succession of substantial structural evidence from at least the later Bronze Age to the post-broch period.

At the Loch of Huxter, Whalsay (Fig. 53a) the blockhouse (Fig. 53b) facing the causeway is integrated into the ring-wall that surrounds the island, but straight joints preclude determining whether the two were successive or contemporary. An entrance passage through the blockhouse has cells on either side, and reports from the mid-nineteenth century suggest that there was formerly an upper level with galleries. The two circular features in the interior are relatively modern structures, though they may overlie original foundations that were contemporary with the fort's Iron Age occupation.

Figure 51: Ness of Burgi, Dunrossness, Shetland.

Figure 52: Clickhimin, Lerwick, Shetland.

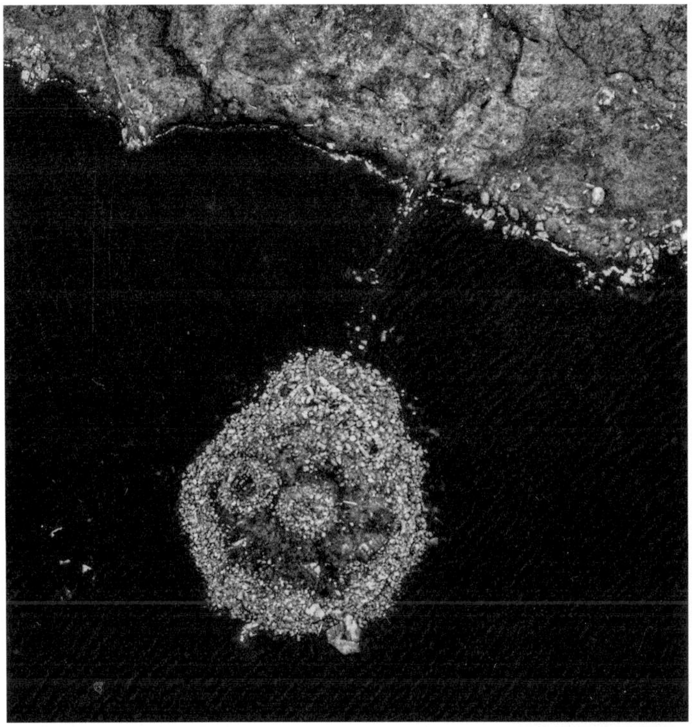

Figure 53a: Loch of Huxter, Whalsay, Shetland.

Loch of Huxter, Whalsay, Shetland, blockhouse façade.

Figure 54: Hog Island, Nesting, Shetland.

In the naturally precipitous terrain of coastal Shetland defensive works needed only to be minimal. In the case of Hog Island, Nesting, (Fig. 54) the narrow neck or natural arch that must once have linked the island to the mainland to create a promontory fort has completely eroded away, and today the island is virtually inaccessible. Its original form, however, is indicated by a stone rampart on the island side of the intervening chasm, which overlooks from a greater height three low banks on the landward side, one now itself virtually eroded by the sea. An entrance gap through the middle of these banks evidently led across the now missing causeway to the island, where the flanking rampart, fifteen metres above the sea, seems largely redundant other than as a breastwork for defenders. The eroded character of the approach to the centre of the island would have permitted further short cross-walls had further defence been necessary, but no trace of such is in evidence.

Some of the Shetland forts occupy truly awe-inspiring locations. Burgi Geos (Fig. 55,a,b) is precipitous to the point that must have made occupation hazardous, and the surrounding landscape of deep peat would probably have been no more attractive to settlement in the Iron Age than it is today. Access is by a narrow spine flanked on the north by a line of boulders, perhaps the residual revetment of

Figure 55a: Burgi Geos, Yell, Shetland. (The structures are left of centre on the main promontiory.)

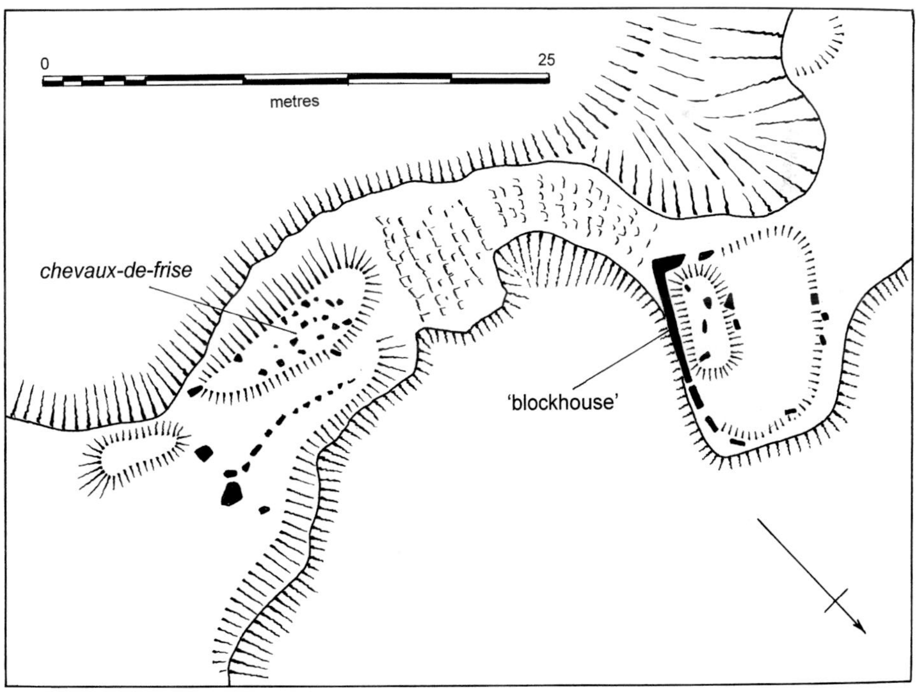

Figure 55b: Burgi Geos, Yell, Shetland, sketch plan of principal features. Drawing by D. W. Harding adapted from Lamb, 1980.

an eroded bank, and on the south by a bank studded with boulders in the manner of a *chevaux-de-frise*. Descending across a saddle the ridge rises on the seaward side to face a blockhouse-like structure with a ring-wall behind it extending round the northern cliff edge. Not surprisingly, there is no evidence of habitation on the promontory. Lamb (1980) was doubtless right in believing that these structures were not intended as a serious defence, but were designed to flank a formal approach to the site, perhaps for prestige, but in this remote and inhospitable location we must suspect also for ceremonial or ritual purposes.

Many of these structures have suffered from stone-robbing in the past or the depredations of antiquarian investigations. Few have benefited from systematic modern research excavation. Of those that have, like the Old Scatness broch complex, the rewards in terms of a better understanding of the origins and development of these important Iron Age sites, and their post-broch sequences into the period of Norse settlement, has been immense. The logistics of mounting an excavation in some of the more remote or inaccessible locations would of course be daunting, and the problems in principle as well as in practice of investigating monuments where unstable stonework is substantially upstanding are not inconsiderable. They are, nevertheless, subject to erosion and progressive decay, so that our failure to investigate will inevitably result in the loss of information and eventually of the sites themselves.

Figure 56: the author with Lima Echo around 1970 at Sunderland airport.

3

Retrospect: Number One to Final

The first time I flew to Orkney I contrived to violate a Purple Airway, a cardinal transgression in the aviator's manual, for which I can only offer the excuse that Her late Majesty the Queen Mother was well behind her published schedule and the Air Traffic Controller who should have warned me off had deserted his post to shake the royal hand. The expedition, which was intended as an archaeological air-photographic survey of Orcadian and Shetland brochs, began auspiciously enough when we set out from Sunderland, reporting at Wick before crossing the Pentland Firth. We had used a technique *en route* that we called 'strap hanging', which involved following the airways to Aberdeen but five hundred feet below its base, because I was not airways qualified. Air Traffic Control invariably spotted that we were obeying the airways rules, so expedited our transit through controlled airspace as if we were qualified, which saved a lengthy detour. I had been aware from the daily bulletins that the Queen Mother was due to open the renovated St Magnus Cathedral at Kirkwall that day in 1974, but the restricted airway was due to be lifted before we arrived at Wick. Evidently the fascination of the occasion, or perhaps a disregard for time which is endemic to island life, resulted in her royal schedule being extended, as a result of which I found myself orbiting Wick, in mounting frustration awaiting clearance from Air Traffic Control to proceed.

In due course clearance was issued, though the restriction on Kirkwall had not been lifted, as became apparent when an aircraft in the silver and red colours of the Queen's Flight became clearly visible still on the ground in front of the terminal buildings at Kirkwall. Radio calls to Kirkwall control failed to elicit any response, as evidently the controller, not anticipating any such breach of air regulations, had joined the presentation party on the tarmac. We flew high overhead and tracked north, hoping the brass band would drown the sound of our intrusion. Some minutes later we heard the captain of Kittihawk Two announcing his departure intentions, and shortly afterwards the distinguished visitor was lifting over the threshold and climbing away to her royal highness of 2500 feet *en route* south. After a respectable pause, I announced my imminent arrival, inbound from the north, hoping the controller would not enquire my point of departure, given the range of a light aircraft of this type. He seemed amiable enough as I entered the control room to pay my landing fee, and I was surprised when he announced that he would need to work out the bill in a few days' time and forward it by post. 'What's there to work out', I asked, 'surely it's the standard Civil Aviation Authority rate of £15?' 'Aye', he replied thoughtfully. 'That's when the airport's open. We close at 5.30, and you landed at 5.45.' 'Yes, I know that.' I was becoming impatient. 'But *we* know the airport was still open, because Herself just left.' 'Quite so,' he replied quietly, 'and the regulations state quite clearly that when the airport is required to be open after hours, the total cost shall be shared between those aircraft using the facility. Do you see my point?' I looked around at the small battalion of police, the fire-tenders and red-carpet rollers, and began to see his point only too well.

A fortnight later I received an account for £15, and learned my first lesson in Orcadian humour. Evidently the royal presence had not distracted his eye from the sight of a small aeroplane flying high overhead through restricted airspace.

My regular colleagues on air-photographic flights for many years when I was based in Durham were two. Denis Ord, my co-pilot, was a natural seat-of-the-pants pilot who could position the aircraft while I was taking photographs as if he were my Siamese twin. He had been a deep-sea diver and also had marine qualifications on sailing ships. Bearded, and invariably wearing a sailor's cap, he gave a passable imitation of King George V at Cowes. In 1984 he survived the sinking of the *Marques* in the West Indies, and we later met up again when he had docked at Leith as master of the replica *Golden Hind*. Our navigator, Raymond Selkirk, also had marine as well as aviation qualifications as a navigator. He had worked with airlines in that capacity, and had a rich seam of politically-incorrect stories about his airlines experiences overseas. I particularly enjoyed his account of flying into Cairo, only to find on the down-wind checks that he had packed the passport in which he had Israeli authorizations rather than the one he used for entering Arab countries, which presented him with a serious dilemma, since neither would accept a passport stamped by the other. In desperation he had proffered at customs his Advanced Laundry book, which in those days bore an impressive embossed emblem on the front cover, and watched the customs officer's puzzled expression as he turned over pages listing shirts and underwear, before finally stamping the book and solemnly returning it. The humour of the tale was not simply the fact that he was able to enter Egypt on a laundry book, but the reaction of the British customs authorities at Heathrow when he tried to pass off the same document on his return, with the comment, 'If it's good enough for....' He was able to gain re-entry, of course, by using his passport that had the Israeli visa and stamps, but the customs officials confiscated his laundry book to add to their unofficial museum of faked documents. History does not relate whether Ray ever recovered his shirts and underwear from the Advanced Laundry. His most recent professional experience had been as a senior air traffic controller, a qualification which proved an immense asset on more than one occasion in our air-photographic sorties. To this he had as a mature student added a degree in Archaeology once he had taken early retirement in his forties from the Civil Aviation Authority. For him, aerial archaeology was almost a third career, though one with greater relaxation than Air Traffic Control or navigating oil tankers across the globe. As he put it in clipped Geordie tones as we levelled out at cruising height one delightful summer's day, 'it beats wor-kin'.' Amen to that!

Leaving the Kirkwall control tower, we headed into town towards the Ayre hotel, where we had been recommended to stay by one of my co-pilot's friends in the oil fraternity, and to convey regards to Grandma Matches, should we encounter her. At first we were told the hotel was full, but mention of Grandma Matches' name seemed to do the trick, and we were directed along the harbour front to a large white house, which evidently served as an annexe for those who knew the password. We had been told to go up to the first floor, where our rooms would be ready, as indeed they were, and that Grandma would appear in due time. We unpacked, and made ourselves at home. After a while, a key turned in a lock in the corridor opposite, a door creaked open, and an elderly lady appeared to enquire our credentials. The presence of a professional diver excited some initial suspicion-we had noted a large brass telegraph from a First World War German dreadnought hanging in the hall- but we persuaded her that our intentions were archaeological and not salvage. Thus appeased, Grandma retired again to her quarters, and we turned our attention to the serious business of planning the following days' sorties.

The residents' lounge at the Ayre was quite full. Our schedule was to be a busy one, with contingency plans for the inevitable unpredictability of the weather. By midnight the bar was still open, and given the variability of licensing hours at that time, I enquired out of curiosity when the bar closed. The barmaid seemed uncomprehending of my question, so I repeated it slowly, as if addressing a foreigner with limited English. 'When... does the bar...close?' She thought for a moment, with a quizzical expression on her face. 'I'm not sure...October, I think', she finally offered. Evidently, it was a question not often asked in these parts.

Air photography around the islands proved physically quite tiring, flying at low height in a succession of steep turns, often along the shoreline where turbulence could be an added hazard. Storms regularly disrupted the prepared itinerary and, as we discovered on this and subsequent expeditions, bad weather could threaten to clamp down and leave us grounded for days on end. We could spend hours poring over weather charts and checking hourly print-outs of forecasts in the Kirkwall met room, seeking some faint glimmer of hope for an improvement in the pattern of low-pressure areas and their attendant drizzle and zero cloud-base. But our hopeful enquiries would inevitably be dashed by the senior met officer, on whose face pessimism seemed etched like the isobars on his weather charts. When the clouds lifted and the sun broke through to afford sufficient contrast in the landscape to warrant photography, our activity became frenetic. One of the targets was the Brough of Birsay, where my colleague at Durham University, Chris Morris (who later became Vice-Principal at Glasgow University shortly after I had stood down as Vice-Principal at Edinburgh), was excavating a Viking-period settlement. We had arranged with him to fly a low pass over the site to signal our readiness to photograph, whereupon he would evacuate his team from their trenches to give maximum exposure to the archaeological features. We arrived only minutes ahead of the next storm, so I handed over the controls to Denis, and asked him to exercise a low pass while I prepared the cameras. The normal execution of this manoeuvre might entail a steady progress over the site at something between 100 and 200 feet, but Denis's approach was more direct. Preferring a steep dive to the copybook gliding descent, he allowed our airspeed to mount rapidly towards the red sector, before pulling the nose upwards and over the cliffs at no more than fifty feet. The effect on the excavation team proved the antithesis to that intended. Instead of evacuating the trenches, they flung themselves in for dear life. I was told later that the finds superintendent, sitting in the site office, had nearly suffered cardiac arrest when looking up to see an aircraft briefly framed in the doorway. The message thus delivered, we climbed back to 600 feet to commence the photographic detail.

On days when flying was not practicable, we toured the islands in a hired car, visiting the archaeological sites we had photographed, and other notable spectacles like the wreck of the *Irene*, which had grounded during a storm on the night when the Longhope lifeboat was lost. One morning we were strolling along the quay at Kirkwall when Denis' attention was drawn to an oil support vessel moored alongside, on which there was a decompression chamber that seemed to excite his interest. There was no-one on deck at that moment, and with his eyes fixed firmly on the external gauges, he suddenly leapt over the rail and began adjusting the controls. The crew alerted, an animated discussion ensued in a language which seemed to be a hybrid of Danish and Geordie, from which it transpired that a disaster had been narrowly averted; as a one-time victim of the bends himself, Denis was only too aware of the dangers of accelerated decompression. Shortly afterwards, we found ourselves below decks enjoying the hospitality and camaraderie of the crew of what must have been one of the very few 'wet' vessels operating in the North Sea. The hospitality was as fulsome as it was insistent, and several hours later we emerged blinking into the daylight, perhaps relieved that the weather was no more fit for flying than we were.

Our programme in Orkney was completed, and with a reasonable weather outlook we determined to fly on to Shetland to continue the air-photographic survey there. The evening before departure, we returned the hire-car to the local garage, refilled it with petrol and paid the balance due. At this point the proprietor realized that we were planning to fly out in the morning, and offered the use of the car to cover the four mile journey to the airport, where he said we could leave the keys with his brother, who ran the taxi service. His trusting good nature appealed to me, and perhaps mischievously I asked how he could be sure we would not spend the rest of the evening cavorting round the island on a free tank of petrol before leaving it empty at the airport. He was sure we would not contemplate any such thing, he replied; and, in any event, if we did, we would not get off the island without paying, because his cousin was the check-in clerk for British Airways, and would not allow us to board unless his brother confirmed that the car had been returned in good order. 'But that's where you have miscalculated,' I said smugly, 'because we are not travelling with British Airways. We have a private aircraft.' 'Ah, well,' he sighed. 'Perhaps you have. But then who do you think is the Air Traffic Controller?'

In 1983 on another air-photographic expedition to the Northern Isles we took off from Kirkwall and turned across Scapa Flow, climbing to set course for Sumburgh. Below us the water was still and clear, and for the only time I ever flew in the Northern Isles we could see on the sea-bed the pencil-thin outline of the *Royal Oak*, a thin oil-slick still seeping from her hull. The battleship had been torpedoed with heavy loss of life in the early years of the war by a U-boat that had slipped into the Flow on the surface through the narrows between islands before the Churchill causeways were built. I still regret not photographing her when we had the chance, since that picture would probably have had more commercial appeal than any of my archaeological photographs. But time was pressing, and we had the best part of a hundred miles of water to cross before reaching the relative haven of Sumburgh. Ray was as thorough a professional as ever, and I noticed him quietly recording on his charts the position and course of surface vessels; should an engine failure cause us to ditch in the sea, survival time in these waters could be measured in minutes, even in summer, and he was instinctively taking out an insurance policy.

We had all as pilots been instructed in emergency ditching procedure, but for obvious reasons had not had practical training as we had with forced landings on land. The essential difference at sea is that a forced landing is directed along the swell, rather than into wind, but stalling the aircraft nose-up on the water to allow some hope of getting out of the cabin and launching a life-raft is an exercise that has more conviction in principle than in practice, and we had all heard stories of crews who had failed to make it. Over a wide expanse of inhospitable water the vulnerability of single-engine flight induces great admiration for the pioneers of aviation, and for us the proverbial airman's aspiration to be the oldest rather than the bravest had much to commend it. We passed over Fair Isle, a barren island set in a sullen sea, and could make out Sumburgh Head in the distance. Sumburgh had prospered during the oil boom, and its terminal buildings displayed internal pretensions beyond most island airports, though externally it was designed like a fortress against hostile storms. The runway was likewise bolstered against the sea with massive concrete blocks that threatened to punish any misjudgement on the part of the approaching pilot. But in good weather, the islands measure up to the tourist's post-card image of seals and puffins, and a summer sun that hardly ever sets.

The archaeological monuments of Shetland are imposing by any standard. Hard by the airport is the site of Jarlshof- a name devised by Sir Walter Scott in *The Pirate* for the tower-house that was built over the prehistoric and Viking settlements. While I was photographing the Iron Age buildings, I could see Ray walking purposefully up and down the grassland beyond, where hundreds of storm petrels had gathered. 'Did you realize,' he began, as if about to make some profound observation, 'that they follow the same procedure for a cross-wind take-off that we do?' He had evidently found that by walking from upwind towards a flock of petrels, they would not take off into wind directly towards him, but diverted sideways with wings dipped into wind. This was evidently preferable to a down-wind take-off, which greatly extends the take-off run, and, as he opined with feigned sagacity, was probably not attainable with a petrel engine. Even more spectacular than Jarlshof is the broch at Mousa, on an island off the east coast of mainland Shetland, and after two thousand years still standing some forty feet high to its parapet. It stood like a sentinel of a remote past in a landscape that was dominated by the early warning paraphernalia of the late twentieth century. The Cold War traditions evidently still lingered on, and some rusting hulks of Russian trawlers had signs on their upper works of suspiciously sophisticated electronic equipment. When they left their anchorages for open water, it was not long before a Royal Navy vessel also slipped its moorings to follow. Ray was particularly interested, since his last posting at Boulmer in Northumberland had been to monitor the Russian Bears and Bisons that tried to slipstream into UK airspace behind scheduled airliners, and when necessary to alert RAF interceptors.

The flying schedule proved demanding and at times frustrating. Without a special permit we were not allowed to take off before 8.0 am, when the sun was shining by three in the morning. Indeed, it was difficult to sleep with only three or four hours of twilight between dusk and dawn. Inevitably, however, the weather broke and we were forced to run before the storm back to the mainland, and to the ultimate sanctuary of the club-house bar, where, like golfers at the nineteenth hole, airmen's adventures assume that extra dimension which the reality itself can never equal.

* * * * *

I had learned to fly in 1970, at the Sunderland Flying Club before the site was developed for the Nissan motor car factory. With a father who had been in the RAF in the last War, and a grandfather in the RFC in the First World War, I suppose it was inevitable that I should have an urge to acquire my 'wings'. Sunderland had been a First World War airfield, and as a legacy of the Second World War there were still along the runway retractable stone pill-boxes designed improbably against airborne invasion. Like many flying clubs of the period, there was a gung-ho amateurism about the whole establishment, with a mixture of members including enthusiasts who messed about with their small, non-radio home-builds with canvas, dope and piano-wire, *nouveau riche* businessmen who hoped to impress their clients with their small twin-engined 'executive' aircraft, and of course, the non-flying members who, unlike the rest of us, sipped their gs and t with lunch. There were also a couple of ex-wartime pilots, who after many years had decided to take up flying once again. It must have been distracting for a brash young instructor, asking a prospective student pilot in later middle age whether he had ever flown before, to receive such a specific response, 'Yes, but not since September 14, 1943, when I was hit by flak over Holland...' The club-house was rather like Michael Caine's dismissive description in the film *Battle of Britain*- 'it leaks and is full of flies' – and sitting in a canvas chair outside, waiting for the weather to improve sufficiently to justify an air-photographic sortie, one felt rather like those earlier pioneers waiting for the order to scramble.

Sunderland airport had its advantages and its disadvantages. There was no scheduled airline traffic like Newcastle to compete with, but correspondingly services were more limited. Located by the coast, it was vulnerable to the ever-threatening sea-fret that could roll inland and blanket the airfield in fog in a matter of minutes. On more than one occasion I assisted Mac the fireman in putting out goose-neck flares along the runway for the benefit of overdue aircraft. Its coastal situation, nevertheless, could be an asset, in that in bad weather one need only fly east to the coast, where it was then safe to descend virtually to sea level in all but the worst visibility. We all then knew how to locate the mouth of the Wear and a small island just offshore in line with the main runway, from which point a compass bearing of 230 degrees would ensure a direct course to the airfield, providing you remembered to climb and count to ten to clear the intervening hill. In fine weather the Penshaw monument, that classical folly on the hill around which the Lambton Worm in legend and folk-song wrapped itself, stood out for miles as a more effective beacon than ADF or VOR. The fact that Sunderland had no scheduled airline traffic was no doubt the reason why a military Buccaneer, suffering a bird strike over the North Sea that shattered the canopy, temporarily blinding the instructor, chose it as an emergency landing field, causing momentary mayhem among the local traffic. The American trainee, flying from the rear seat, landed impeccably, though inevitably running into the fence at the far end of the relatively short runway, and closing the airport whilst security men flooded the area, not least, we understood, because the aircraft was armed. As a splendid PR gesture, the squadron leader instructor (later to become Air Commodore) subsequently agreed to present the club's new pilots with their 'wings' at the annual passing-out party.

Only once was I really caught out by a combination of low cloud and sea-fret, when photographing in the Tweed valley. Ray's experience as a former Air Traffic Controller now came into its own, and he firmly instructed me to climb through the cloud to avoid any possible hill or obstruction while he checked that Newcastle radar was operational. This facility, of course, was only available strictly to pilots with the appropriate rating, which I had not. He turned to me and asked if I could fly to within two degrees and fifty feet, which I assured him I could. As a former airways controller, he obviously knew the jargon, and proceeded to relay with translation the ground controller's instructions to me. As we joined the approach pattern over Newcastle in intense cloud and rain I could see nothing, but with the bearings given and a progressive descent it was obvious that we were on the final approach. 'Lima Echo, you are number one to final', said a calming voice from the control tower. At three hundred feet the visibility cleared marginally, and I could see the runway lights directly ahead. 'It's all yours', announced my navigator, 'stick it down'. We landed in a shower of spray, and taxied to the apron. We paid our landing fee, and no-one even queried whether our double-act might have been less than legitimate.

Instructors tended to be birds of passage, never staying very long in one posting. They were either young men acquiring hours in order to advance a career in commercial aviation, or older men, retiring relatively early from a career in the airlines. I remember particularly one of the latter, a retired KLM captain, who taught me an alternative approach to cross-wind landings, which he claimed to have performed with a DC9. The standard procedure was to approach the runway crab-wise, with nose into wind, in order to ensure a direct track towards the runway. In the final stages of round-out, one then straightened the aircraft with rudder and counteracted the consequences with opposite stick, holding the into-wind wing down to avoid flipping over. The KLM method was more direct. It simply involved side-slipping the aircraft into the wind while holding a direct course for the runway, straightening up, of course, before the into-wind wing struck the runway. Side-slipping was strictly discouraged among trainee pilots, presumably because it was a potentially dangerous manoeuvre, but my father had insisted I should learn how to do it, as it was the quickest way of descending, and the safest if one's Spitfire's engine was on fire, as the side-slip would carry the flames away from the canopy. Another of my instructors, who would probably have agreed, was an ex-RAF pilot based at Teesside Airport, who suffered from what was called the fighter pilot's twitch, a nervous affliction which caused an involuntary grimace every few seconds as he briefed his trainees for their next exercise. It was an unnerving experience that certainly did not inspire confidence as one walked across the tarmac with him to the aircraft. It was uncanny, therefore, how the twitch disappeared with the cry of 'contact' and the firing of the engines: by the time the aircraft was lifting off the runway his face had relaxed, and his expression conveyed confidence and experience that was immensely reassuring.

My instructor during training had been a local lad, with laconic Wearside sense of humour. I remember being taught the procedure for recovery from stalls and spins by him, which involved climbing to a safe height and location, shutting off power, pulling the nose up until the aircraft shuddered in the stall, then kicking it with rudder into a spin. Recovery was expected to be implemented immediately, but I was barely conscious of the spinning sensation, and evidently left the aircraft in the spin for several revolutions. 'How many cows are there in that field?' my instructor quietly enquired. 'How many...? What? I don't know,' I stumbled. 'Well,' said he a little more urgently, 'you'll be able to get out and count them for yourself if you don't pull this bloody thing out!' If you have ever thought that being a driving instructor must induce more nervous breakdowns than most professions, how much truer must this be of flying instructors. This one relaxed on the way home from a detail by practising barrel-rolls, perhaps as a measure of repayment to his errant pupils for all the grief they had caused him. I was never sick in the air, and generally simply went into semi-detached mode while he performed his aerobatics. Only on one occasion did I try to follow what he was doing by focusing alternately on instruments and horizon, whereupon a wave of nausea swept over me, and I abandoned the idea. On one other occasion I experienced a similar feeling. It was when he said he would show me why one should not fly into cloud unnecessarily. Through broken cloud he circled a television mast west of Newcastle, and there I could see steps leading from the summit right the way to the ground. Looking at the ground from the air is not unlike looking at a map. But seeing steps leading from the wing-tip to the ground is a very nauseating sensation.

Though non-radio aircraft were permitted at Sunderland, there was a proper procedure for joining overhead for non-radio aircraft, with instructions for landing flashed by coloured lamp. So I was surprised one day standing in the Control Tower to hear the duty controller urgently instruct an aircraft on final approach to abort, on the grounds of a conflicting aircraft landing on an intersecting runway. We duly identified it as a Hornet Moth, and the pilot, who was ushered into the clubhouse by a group of very sceptical Geordie members, proved to be Marion Wilberforce, sister of the law lord who had conducted the enquiry into the 1972 miners' strike. She was of the Amy Johnson generation of pioneer women aviators, and had flown the Moth since the 1930s. She had just returned from Norway, where evidently she had put the cat among the pigeons by landing unannounced at a military airfield in order the get a faulty magneto replaced. The club members, many of whom had never flown beyond the local area on a Sunday afternoon, were duly tickled by her old-fashioned manners, and asked her naughtily if she had ever flown any other aircraft. Oh yes, she replied, certainly she had. The Spitfire and Hurricane she had quite enjoyed flying, but the Lancaster she found rather heavy for her. The complacent amusement on the faces of the amateur pilots around her evaporated. She had been a ferry pilot during the War in the Air Transport Auxiliary, and had infinitely more air experience than any of us. Most of us had only ever seen these aircraft in museums or at air shows, though I had actually once encountered a Battle of Britain display flight in the air. Momentarily stunned by the sight of a Spitfire and Messerschmitt Bf109 flanking in formation a third aircraft that from our wartime childhood we recognized from its distinctive rear-facing upper gun turret as a Boulton Paul Defiant, I had been slow to grab the cameras, and another memorable photograph joined the ranks of those that got away. Marion's Moth had been refuelled, and it was time for her to leave. Getting down from her stool she asked, 'anyone give me a swing?' and disappeared on to the tarmac surrounded by admiring volunteers.

* * * * *

Sea-fret was not the only natural hazard; flying in upland areas or among the Border hills at low altitude in steep turns for photography, turbulence and wind-sheer were potentially dangerous. In training in good conditions and in anticipation of the manoeuvre it was perfectly possible to pull a light aircraft out of a spin in five hundred feet. But the unpredictable conditions in the hills were a different matter, and we frequently were operating below that threshold. A related hazard was illustrated by the expedition to photograph the Roman camp of Whitley Castle, near Alston in Cumbria (Fig. 10), which provided a salutary lesson in aviation. The South Tyne valley lies on a north-south axis, and the site was on its west side, at around 1100 feet on a hillside that rises to over 1500 feet at its summit. Orbiting the target at 600 feet the aircraft must have been around a thousand feet above the valley bottom; turning anticlockwise westwards, the clearance over the hills was inevitably much less. Every pilot is aware of the fact that prevailing winds in Britain are south-westerly, and equally every trained pilot is familiar with the possible effects of 'wind sheer' over hilly terrain. On this occasion the down draught in the lee of the hills was so strong that, even with full power applied and the control stick pulled back hard into the stomach, the altimeter was spiraling downwards, demanding a steep turn to avoid by a nerve-wracking margin a premature and unplanned landing on the moorland. The experience concentrated the mind to ensure that a single orbit was sufficient to achieve the required results.

The risks of low flying, however, were not confined to the weather. The north of England and the Borders include several military ranges, into which aircraft on exercises had a habit of flying quite quickly and quite low. A pair of RAF pilots once confided that they practised repeatedly out at sea until they could cross the cliffs at Hartlepool flat out at fifty feet on their way to the Barnard Castle range. In the Border valleys military aircraft attacked targets in the Otterburn range hugging the valley floor at maximum speed. On one unforgettable occasion four such fighters flew *beneath* me when I was orbiting at three hundred feet over Woden Law, causing considerable wake turbulence. The first warning I had was seeing the shadow of the leading aircraft pass over the ground in front of the aircraft itself, enough to induce in any pilot a reaction akin to that of a sparrow detecting the imminence of a hawk. To make matters worse, the pilot of the lead aircraft from his expression seemed to find the incident amusing. It was the one occasion in my flying career when I was moved to report a near miss. The regional controller seemed sceptical, and asked for my estimate of the separation between us. I responded that I found it hard to judge, but I could tell him that the military pilot's name, inscribed on his helmet, was monosyllabic, like Reid, or something very similar. There was a momentary pause- I fancied a metaphorical drawing-in of breath- before the controller confirmed that this would indeed rank as a near miss, and that he would advise other traffic in the region.

Operating on the fringes of the military zone always risked being warned off by controllers, though I believe we never once intruded without permission. I was several times told by assertive controllers that I was inside the boundaries, but was able to give an eight figure national grid reference to verify our actual location. Accuracy in site identification and location meant navigating by farms and by-ways to a level seldom required in flight navigation. There were, of course, archaeological sites of interest within the range, and accordingly I sought permission to overfly when exercises were not in progress. I was put in contact with the Range Liaison Officer, who at that time was a captain with a double-barreled name that I have now forgotten, but whom I imagined was more interested in the local hunt than his military advancement. At that time we were flying a high wing, wooden and canvas aircraft called a Brochet, which had a fuselage like a banana and expansive high wings that resulted in a stall speed as low as thirty miles an hour, which meant that flying into wind it might virtually have been capable of hovering over the target site. My co-owners of this unique piece of aviation history used it for charitable events and displays, and accordingly it was brightly painted in black and white chequer-board squares with yellow leading edges, and with black Maltese crosses on the wings. I had explained this to the Range Liaison Officer, expressing my ardent hope that his gunners would not mistake the Brochet for a target drone. In his reply he assured me that there was no risk whatsoever. 'As to your technicolor aeroplane', he wrote, 'let me assure you that our gunners could not hit it, even if you landed it on the ends of their gun-barrels....'

Surely enough, the demise of the Brochet was not through artillery barrage. I remember one night having a nightmare, in which I dreamt that it had crashed beyond repair. I could not work out whether I was involved, but the dream was so vivid that early the following morning I drove to the airfield before anyone was about, and looked in through a hangar window. To my relief and embarrassment, there it was, quite unmarked and undamaged, and sheepishly I drove back to my nine o'clock lecture. One week later, Denis inexplicably got caught in a rogue down-draught at low height and crashed the plane in west Durham; he and his passenger survived unscathed, but the plane was a write-off.

* * * * *

When Sunderland airport closed, my Geordie crew and I continued to operate together for a while from Newcastle, but commuting became progressively inconvenient for us all, as by this time I was based in Edinburgh. As late as 1983 we were meeting up at Milfield where we used the deserted RAF airfield as a base for early morning survey in the Cheviots. A six-thirty take-off in April to catch the first half-hour of hoar frost meant an early departure from Edinburgh, but the results were rewarding, provided that the weather turned out as forecast. Otherwise we would sit in the transport café in Milfield village eating bacon butties before embarking on the joyless return journey. The only problem, one that eventually brought our operations to an end, was that Milfield aerodrome was being progressively quarried away, and each time we arrived the only usable runway was a few yards shorter. Furthermore, the quarry company had an irritating habit of leaving their drag-line with its boom pointing skywards right at the end of the truncated runway, so that landing required side-slipping the aircraft before executing a very sharp turn on to the tarmac followed by sharp breaking to avoid going through the fence at the end. Likewise we gained plenty of practice in short field take-offs, winding up power whilst holding the aircraft on its brakes, before releasing it like a hare out of the trap. Eventually we were overtaken by the inevitable, and my early morning forays came to an end.

By now I had in any event joined a new flying club at Glenrothes. In retrospect, it seems that my membership was some kind of blight upon otherwise thriving organizations, since it too in due course closed down. I have noticed the same fate afflicts manufacturers of clothes, shoes or a multitude of domestic tools and equipment, all of whom seem prone to bankruptcy or take-over the moment I take a liking to their products. Only my Edinburgh tailor seems to have survived the jinx. On the first occasion I purchased a suit from him I remarked jocularly that this was bound to ensure his business's demise, to which he frostily observed that they had been making gentlemen's suits since the 1720s (in his case I could believe it as his bent, spectral figure hovered about me with a tape-measure) and that they had no intention of ceasing to do so in the foreseeable future. Happily they remained in business in Queen's Street until long after I had retired. At Glenrothes I was fortunate to have the services and companionship of George Ballingall, an ex-RAF pilot who had genuinely started his career on Spitfires, as my partner on air-photographic expeditions. From Spitfire George I learned a number of wrinkles of airmanship, not least how to cope with a magneto electrical failure, which was the selfsame problem that had led to my making a forced landing at Sunderland after it had officially closed. On the first occasion I had been alerted to the problem by the fact that the ignition warning light stayed on, but I was unaware that there was anything I could do to conserve the battery from draining flat. Progressively the instruments failed, then the radio, which prevented our returning to Newcastle, where non-radio aircraft were not permitted to mix with commercial traffic. Uncertain whether even the flaps would function on landing, I had headed back to Sunderland, now derelict but not yet developed, where we were met with a less than rapturous welcome by the security guards. The key to salvation, as I learnt from Spitfire George, was quite simply to switch off the master switch, which surprisingly perhaps does not cause the aircraft to stop flying, though it does immobilize all the instruments, including of course, the radio. It is therefore advisable to inform the appropriate controller of one's intention before doing so, and to agree a later rendezvous when the residual power in the battery can be switched back on for the vital purposes of landing.

Apart from visits to the Northern Isles, I had also flown to Stornoway on more than one occasion, the first time in 1984 from Teesside. Diversionary fields in the event of bad weather are few and far between on the west side of Scotland, but fortunately the main stop-over point for refuelling, Prestwick, had a reputation for remaining open three hundred and sixty-four days in the year. Its long runways, on which I could have landed and taken off at least three times without running out of tarmac, and more especially its huge white hangars, were visible from miles away, providing a beacon of comfort to the private pilot returning from the inhospitable environment of the Minch and Inner Hebrides. But long runways betoken large or very fast aircraft, and manoeuvring a single-engined Cessna in landing or take-off behind a jumbo jet required extreme vigilance to avoid the potentially fatal hazard of wake turbulence, which could remain a danger for a very long time after the aircraft's departure. It was crucial to note the point of lift-off and to ensure that one's own take-off preceded this point by a sufficient margin to divert well to one side before climbing away. Wake turbulence could be produced by helicopters too, and Ray warned me on an early visit to Prestwick to steer well clear of departing helicopters. Even on the ground it was unwise to taxi too close behind a transatlantic airliner, though I was always treated with courtesy and consideration by commercial pilots. I recall an American pilot being advised by Air Traffic Control at Prestwick that I was behind him at the holding point. 'Hullo, little aeroplane' drawled a friendly voice, hardly in accordance with formal RT procedure. 'What's your name?' 'Lima Echo', I replied, giving the Cessna's abbreviated call sign. 'That's a *nice* name,' continued the voice. 'We'll try not to blow you away...'

I had first stopped over at Prestwick in 1979, en route to Islay. It was then that I first experienced the problems of judging height on approach to landing over peat bog, where the sombre colours and lack of clearly-defined structures played tricks on the eyes, especially in the squally weather conditions that were prevailing on my first visit to Port Ellen. Through a rain storm of quite sudden intensity the end of the runway was lit by brilliant shafts of sunlight through breaks in the cloud. I remember the controller asking if I wished to abort the landing and go round again, but I was already committed to landing, and touched down in a cloud of spray. Waiting on the apron was an Andover of the Queen's Flight, prudently having decided to wait a few moments until the squall passed. I climbed the control tower steps to pay my landing fee, admiring the tomato plants growing in the windows; the expanse of glass in a Control Tower, designed, one might presume, to give controllers a clear and unimpeded view of aircraft, was obviously ideal for amateur horticulture. Enquiring the identity of the royal visitor, I was assured that it was none other than the newly-elected Prime Minister, Margaret Thatcher, who seemingly regularly visited the island as a summer retreat.

The Western Isles could be equally unpredictable in terms of weather. Unlike the standard A-shape of airfields in Britain, in which three main runways offered six options depending upon the wind direction, Stornoway originally had eight. At the time of my first visit the main runway was being modified to accommodate NATO jets, and furthermore the subordinate runways were out of commission. Room for manoeuvre therefore was somewhat restricted, particularly in a cross-wind. Pausing at the checkpoint I asked the controller which direction of the main runway was in use. Take your choice, he replied, since the wind was at 90 degrees to the track anyway. I turned to Ray for advice. One way the sea was directly beyond the end of the runway; the other way steamrollers and contractor's lorries blocked the end of the track. 'I'd opt for the sea', Ray volunteered. Around the islands the coastline was very different, the rocky inlets and lochs on the east contrasting with the long, sandy beaches on the west. One could have landed a light aircraft in an emergency on the sands at Uig, where the Norse chessmen were found, or on the extensive beaches of the southern islands. In fact, of course, there were regular flights in and out of Barra, where the runway was the beach and where we were told that the pilot's first enquiry of the local controller therefore was whether the plug was out. There was, of course, another runway, again very long and forbidding within its military exclusion zone, on Benbecula, but here I never had occasion to land. The problem with aerial survey in the Western Isles, of course, was always the weather; it was a long way to fly and expensive in aircraft hire, only to find that conditions were unsuitable for air photography.

With George I flew on a number of occasions in quite marginal conditions in the hills, where turbulence and low cloud was an ever-present hazard. I recall returning with him from the Western Isles, and instead of following the longer coastal route home we cut through the Highland valleys, following a route that he remembered using when flying Hunters, which involved slipping from one glen to the next through narrow clefts in the mountain ranges. The key to survival was not to miss a crucial turn, and end up in a 'box canyon', becoming progressively hemmed in by hills under a low cloud base.

When Glenrothes closed I flew occasionally from Turnhouse at Edinburgh. But already by the mid-nineties it was becoming clear that major airports found private aviation a tiresome interference with the more important business of commercial aviation. Air traffic procedure like every other branch of administration was becoming increasingly bureaucratic, and Edinburgh, not the busiest airport in Britain, now had a Ground Controller, as well as Tower and Approach Controllers, through each of whose jurisdiction with change of frequency one passed before leaving the local area for a Regional Controller. 'Patter' was also much more formal. I was once reprimanded for not repeating back wind speed and direction on the final approach, but simply acknowledging with my call-sign. In earlier days I had been taught that in busy traffic a double click on the button was sufficient to indicate 'message received and understood'. As Ray had put it, 'if the controller has half a dozen stacked up behind you waiting for instructions, he doesn't want to hear your life history'. Well, Ray was wrong, God rest him: nowadays, it seems, they do.

4

Colour Plates

Plate 1. Tofts field, Piercebridge, Co. Durham, *vicus* between Dere Street and Roman fort.

Plate 2. Larberry Pastures, Stockton-on-Tees, Co. Durham, native enclosure.

Plate 3. Easter Muirdean, Kelso, Roxburghshire, double-ditched enclosure.

Plate 4. Thornybank, Dalkeith, Midlothian.

Plate 5. Ovingham, Northumberland, ditched enclosure.

Plate 6. A landscape of islands and lochs: the Udal and beyond, North Uist.

Plate 7. Woden Law, Roxburghshire, hillfort, 'siege-works' and linear banks, and palisaded enclosure (bottom, left of centre).

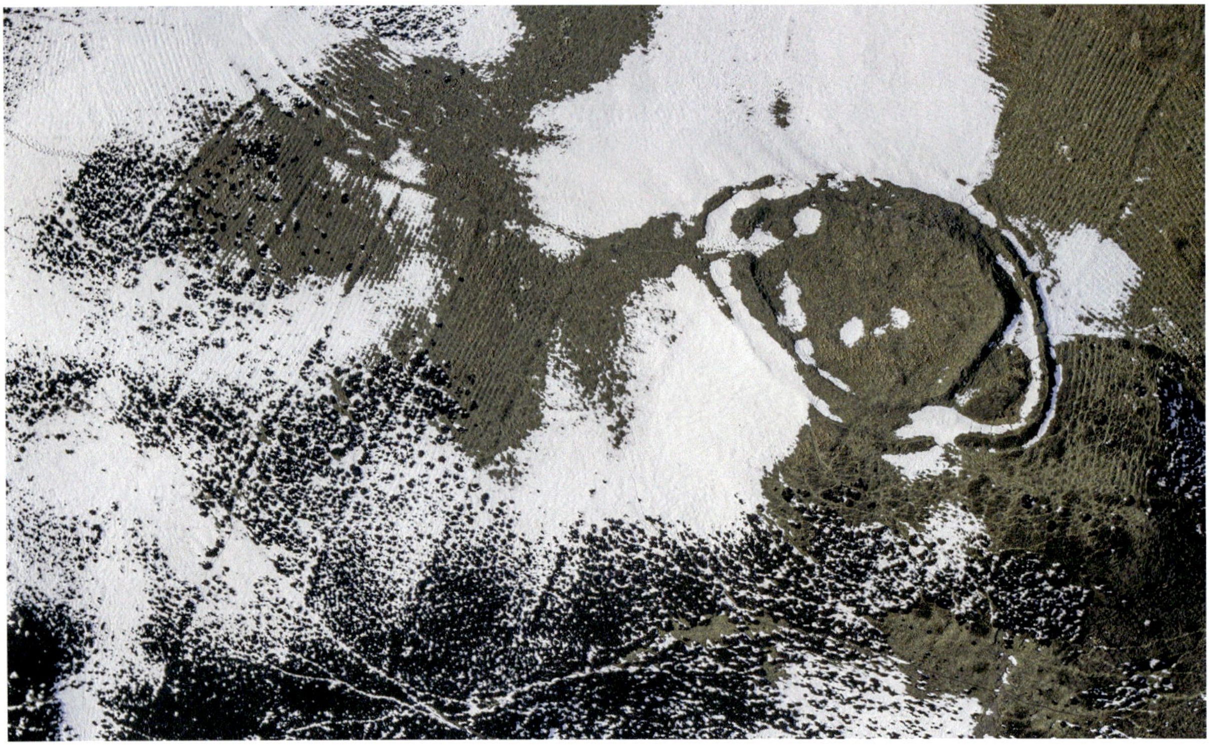

Plate 8a. Hut Knowe, Hownam, Roxburghshire, hillfort and cord-rig fields under snow.

Plate 8b. Hut Knowe, Hownam, Roxburghshire, hillfort and cord-rig fields under heavy frost.

Plate 9. Holme House, Piercebridge (North Yorkshire), ditched enclosure by road.

Plate 10. Hownam Rings, Roxburghshire.

Plate 11. Hownam Law, Roxburghshire.

Plate 12. The Castles, Morebattle, Roxburghshire.

Plate 13. Yeavering Bell, Northumberland.

Plate 14. Carrock Fell, Cumbria.

Plate 15. Blackbrough, Hownam, Roxburghshire, hillfort and palisaded enclosure.

Plate 16. Stanshiel Hill, Hownam,Roxburghshire, large palisaded enclosure.

Plate 17. Thowliestane Hill, Hownam, Roxburghshire, hillfort with outer palisades.

Plate 18. Craik Moor, Morebattle, Roxburghshire, hillfort with ring-ditch houses and outer palisades.

Plate 19a. Stanwick, North Yorkshire, view north-west across Henah Hill.

Plate 19b. Stanwick, North Yorkshire, view south-east across the Tofts and church.

Plate 20. Chesters north and Sixpence Strip, Drem, East Lothian ditched (top, right) and ditched and palisaded (bottom, left) enclosures.

Plate 21. Castle O'er, Dumfriesshire, hillfort.

Plate 22. Bailiehill, Dumfriesshire, hillfort.

Plate 23. Dundurn, Perthshire, nuclear fort.

Plate 24. Hayhope Knowe, Morebattle, Roxburghshire.

Plate 25. Camp Tops, Morebattle, Roxburghshire.

Plate 26. Chesters, Spott, East Lothian, multivallate hillfort.

Plate 27. Sundhope Kip, Hownam, Roxburghshire.

Plate 28. Springhill, Berwickshire, triple-ditched enclosure.

Plate 29. Bemersyde Moss, Berwickshire, double-ditched enclosure beneath agricultural drainage.

Plate 30. High Knowes, Alnham, Northumberland, A, bottom, B, top. Palisaded settlements with ring-ditch houses.

Plate 31. Pudding Law, Morebattle, Roxburghshire, palisaded and banked enclosures, ring-ditch houses and cord-rig agriculture.

Plate 32. Greenbrough, Hownam, Roxburghshire, palisaded settlement.

Plate 33. Broomside, Co. Durham, ditched enclosure.

Plate 34. Brandon, Co. Durham, ditched enclosure.

Plate 35a. Whitecraig, East Lothian, pit-alignment and ditched enclosures.

Plate 35b. Whitecraig, East Lothian, double pit-alignment and palisaded enclosure.

Plate 35c. Whitecraig, East Lothian, pit-alignment and linear ditches.

Plate 36. Whitelaw Hill, East Lothian, pit-alignment and ditched enclosure.

Plate 37. Eilean Breaban, Loch Tay.

Plate 38. Mary's Distaff, Loch Tay.

Plate 39. Craggan, Loch Tay.

Plate 40. Dall Bay, Loch Tay.

Plate 41. Bandry, Loch Lomond.

Plate 42. Cameron Bay, Loch Lomond.

Plate 43. Milton Morenish, Loch Tay.

Plate 44. Fearnan Hotel, Loch Tay.

Plate 45. Mill Cairn, Loch Lomond.

Plate 46. Strathcashel Point, Loch Lomond.

Plate 47a. Loch an Duin, Shader, Lewis.

Plate 47b. Loch an Duin, Shader, Lewis.

Plate 48. Gurness, Mainland, Orkney, broch village.

Plate 49. Midhowe, Rousay, Orkney, broch village.

Plate 50. Loch an Duna, Bragar, Lewis, island broch.

Plate 51a. Borve, Lewis, broch.

Plate 51b. Borve, Lewis, broch, from *c.* 300 feet.

Plate 52. Iona abbey, Inner Hebrides.

Plate 53. Whitby, North Yorkshire.

References

Armit, I. and McKenzie, J. (2013), *An Inherited Place: Broxmouth Hillfort and the South-East Scottish Iron Age*, Edinburgh, Society of Antiquaries of Scotland.

Cavers, G. (2010), *Crannogs and Later Prehistoric Settlement in Western Scotland*, Oxford, BAR British Series 510.

Cook, M. and Dunbar, L. (2008), *Rituals, Roundhouses and Romans, Excavations at Kintore, Aberdeenshire 2000-2006, Volume 1, Forest Road*, Edinburgh, Scottish Trust for Archaeological Research.

Cool, H. and Mason, D. (2008), *Roman Piercebridge, Excavations by D. W. Harding and Peter Scott 1969-1981*, Durham, The Architectural Society of Durham and Northumberland.

Dixon, N. (2007), 'Crannog structure and dating in Perthshire with particular reference to Loch Tay', in Green, C. (ed.), *Archaeology from the Wetlands: Recent Perspectives*, Edinburgh, Society of Antiquaries of Scotland: 253-66.

Dockrill, S. J. Bond, J. M., Turner, V. E., Brown, L. D., Bashford, D. J., Cussans, J. E. and Nicholson, R. A. (2010), *Excavations at Old Scatness, Shetland, Volume 1: The Pictish Village and Viking Settlement*, Lerwick, Shetland Heritage Publications.

Dockrill, S. J. Bond, J. M., Turner, V. E., Brown, L. D., Bashford, D. J., Cussans, J. E. and Nicholson, R. A. (2015), *Excavations at Old Scatness, Shetland, Volume 2: The Broch and Middle Iron Age Village*, Lerwick, Shetland Heritage Publications.

Halliday, S. (1982), 'Later prehistoric farming in south-east Scotland', in Harding, D. W. (ed.), *Later Prehistoric Settlement in South-East Scotland*, Edinburgh, University of Edinburgh Department of Archaeology Occasional Paper No. 8: 75-91.

Harding, A. (1987), *Henge Monuments and Related Sites of Great Britain: air-photographic evidence and catalogue*, Oxford, BAR British Series 175.

Harding, D. W. (2017), *The Iron Age in Northern Britain, Britons and Romans, Natives and Settlers*, Abingdon, Routledge.

____ (2020), *Rewriting History; changing perceptions of the archaeological past*, Oxford, Oxford University Press.

Harding, D. W. and Dixon, T. N. (2000), *Dun Bharabhat, Cnip: An Iron Age Settlement in West Lewis, Vol. 1, Structures and Material Culture*, Edinburgh, Edinburgh University Department of Archaeology.

Harding, D. W. and Gilmour, S. M. D. (2000), *The Iron Age Settlement at Beirgh, Riof, Isle of Lewis: Excavations 1985-1995, Vol. 1, The Structures and Stratigraphy*, Edinburgh, Edinburgh University Department of Archaeology.

Haselgrove, C. (2009), *The Traprain Law Environs Project: Fieldwork and Excavations 2000-2004*, Edinburgh, Society of Antiquaries of Scotland.

Haselgrove, C. (2016), *Cartimandua's Capital: A Late Iron Age Royal Site at Stanwick, North Yorkshire*, London, CBA Research Report 175.

Jobey, G. and Tait, J. (1966), 'Excavations on Palisaded Settlements and Cairnfields at Alnham, Northumberland', *Archaeologia Aeliana*, 4th series, XLIV: 5-48.

Jones, G. D. B. and Woolliscroft, D. (2001), *Hadrian's Wall from the air*, Stroud, Tempus.

Lamb, R. (1980), *Iron Age Promontory Forts in the Northern Isles*, Oxford, BAR British Series 79.

McCord, N. (1971), *Durham History from the Air*, Newcastle upon Tyne, Durham County Local History Society.

____(1972), *Northumberland History from the Air*, Newcastle upon Tyne, Frank Graham.

McMillan, J. (2001), *Air photography in East Lothian and Berwickshire*, unpublished MA Dissertation, Department of Archaeology, University of Edinburgh.

Mercer, R. J. (2018), *Native and Roman on the Northern Frontier: Excavation and Survey in the Later Prehistoric Landscape in Upper Eskdale, Dumfriesshire*, Edinburgh, Society of Antiquaries of Scotland.

Morrison, I. (1985), *Landscape with Lake Dwellings*, Edinburgh, Edinburgh University Press.

Piggott, C. M. (1948), 'Excavations at Hownam Rings, Roxburghshire, 1948', *Proceedings of the Society of Antiquaries of Scotland*, 82, 1947-8: 193-225.

____(1949), 'The Iron Age settlement at Hayhope Knowe, Roxburghshire: excavations, 1949', *Proceedings of the Society of Antiquaries of Scotland*, 83, 1948-9: 45-67.

Piggott, S. (1966). 'A scheme for the Scottish Iron Age', in Rivet, A. L. F. (ed), *The Iron Age in Northern Britain*, Edinburgh, Edinburgh University Press: 1-16.

RCAHMS (1956), *An Inventory of the Ancient and Historical Monuments of Roxburghshire*, Edinburgh, HMSO.

____(1967), *Peeblesshire, an Inventory of the Ancient Monuments*, Edinburgh, HMSO.

Richmond, I. A. and St. Joseph, J. K. (1982), 'Excavations at Woden Law, 1950', *Proceedings of the Society of Antiquaries of Scotland*, 112: 277-84.

Rideout, J., Owen, O. and Halpin, E. (1992), *Hillforts of Southern Scotland*, Edinburgh, Historic Scotland/AOC.

Riley, D. (1987), *Air Photography and Archaeology*, London, Duckworth.

Wheeler, R. E. M. (1954), *The Stanwick Fortifications, North Riding of Yorkshire*, Oxford, Society of Antiquaries of London Research Report 17.

Willis, S. and Carne, P. (2013), *A Roman Villa at the edge of Empire, Excavations at Ingleby Barwick, Stockton-on-Tees, 2003-4*, York, Council for British Archaeology Research Report 170.

Wilson, D. (1982), *Air Photo Interpretation for Archaeologists*, London, Batsford, second edition 2000, Stroud, Tempus.